Unpuzzling Innovation

Mastering Innovation Management in a Structural Way

PEARL ZHU

ISBN: 978-1-387-76426-6 (sc)
ISBN: 978-1-483-358757-8 (e)

Contents

Introduction

Introduction

Digital Innovation is a dynamic storybook that has intricate chapters, with a serendipitous cover, which can be flipped over to the next level, but it is a book that never ends.

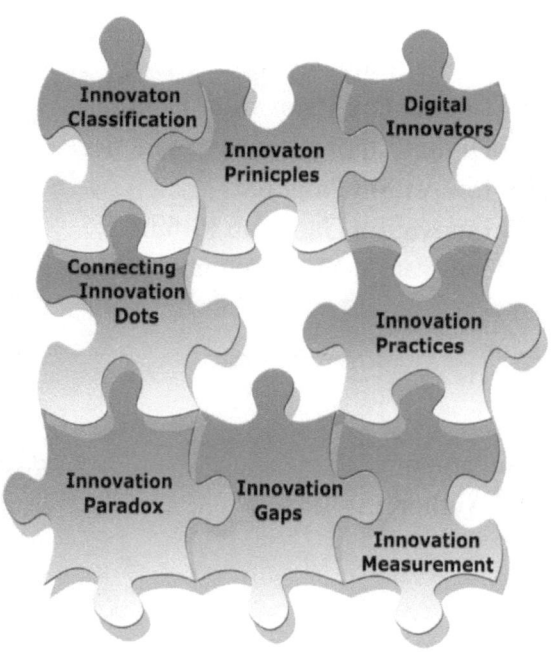

Figure 1 Mastering Innovation Management in a Structural Way

Digital is the age of innovation. And innovation is what leads to differentiation. There are many ways to differentiate and, therefore, there are many ways to pursue innovation. Talking about innovation is not new nowadays, everybody, every organization now is talking about innovation. It's been at or near the top of the business or economics agenda for a long time. However, there're a lot of confusions about innovation and there is no magic sauce to guarantee its success. Back to basic, what is innovation, the more you look into this topic, the more difficult to give a definition of innovation, as it is such a broad topic. One of the good definitions of innovation is: "to transform the novel ideas into commercial success." In essence, innovation is, "intentional novelty bringing sustainable benefit."

- **Innovation is about future**: Without it, you lose sight of tomorrow. Innovation is an exceptional, exclusive, and realistic idea that separates you from others without a second thought.

- **Innovation is about growth**: It captures the essential element of any business and quality within every leader. When innovation outside your organization outraces innovation inside your organization, it is time to address factors influencing business velocity, performance, profitability and customer preference. Look to and listen to your data, use it to help you drive innovation.

- **Innovation is to reinvent business, but not to reinvent the wheels**: Innovation is about reinventing the business direction and purpose at any time. It defines strategy, profitability and relevance at any given time. If you do not, you become commoditized and just like so many others who offer the same product or service. Innovation allows one to stand out and above the rest.

- **Innovation is oxygen**: As with humans and oxygen, businesses cannot survive without innovation. You must differentiate yourself in the marketplace. It is like the air we breathe, it is like the water we drink, it's a natural element to keep us alive.

- **Innovation is a double-edged sword**: Keep aware of it and use both edges to your advantage. Innovation is the creative idea or a quick, alternative way of solving the existing problem with affordable price to the customer. Innovation is also doing the conventional task in an unconventional, simpler, and much more efficient way.

- **Innovation is converting a problem into an opportunity**: The wheel was an innovation that converted the problem of weightlifting and transport into so many vistas of innumerable applications.

- **Innovation is the heart for improvement**: Do something in a new way. Innovation is 'incremental value creation' leveraging simplistic or intricate ideas into reality. It's the unexpected synthesis of an idea, followed by a lot of commitment.

- **Innovation is life; a continuous journey of digital transformation**: It brings new energy, forces you to be at your best at all times. It is an alpha; it is the beginning of all things. It is also timeless - for our minds will never stop.

Creativity is the mental process to create novel ideas, and innovation is to transform novel ideas to achieve their business value. The creativity ingredients include curiosity, knowledge, urge, inspiration, intuition, need and necessity, instinct, survival of the fittest and larger good simple brilliance, boldness, logic, rationality, out of the box thinking, fluidity, flexibility, discovery, stretch, influence, experiment, insight, prioritization, customer-centricity, open-mindedness, transdisciplinarity, inquisitiveness, and risk tolerance, etc. A new idea, a new method, a new product or service, a new business proposition, a new and better deployment of resources, another way to achieve better results, etc, all contribute to innovation.

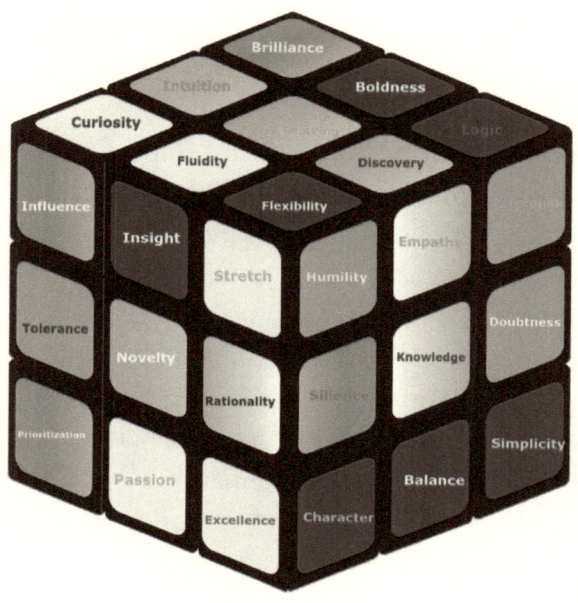

Figure 2 The Creativity Cube

The purpose of **"Unpuzzling Innovation - Mastering Innovation Management in a Structural Way"** is to demystify innovation puzzle in a structural way. Innovation is the process which can be classified scientifically and managed dynamically. Innovation is neither serendipity nor status quo, it is important to break some outdated rules, build digital principles, and take a systematic approach with robust, but not overly rigid processes to implement it. Digital innovators are the "whole-brainers" who present leadership skills and multidimensional intelligence, to mastering the "art of possible." Creativity is simply about connecting the dots, the difference between innovation and creativity is implementation. It's important to develop a set of best/next practices to manage digital innovation continuum effectively. It's also critical to understand the paradox of innovation and strike the right balance between ideation and execution part of the innovation process and management. Innovation journey is thorny, be cautious about gaps and pitfalls on the way, to improve innovation success rate and measure it in the right way. This book intends to:

- Classify digital innovation into a broader spectrum
- Set principles for managing innovation and handling risk in a structural way
- Recognize innovators with creative traits
- Reinvent business direction, models, culture, or products/services/solution
- Manage complex, balanced and dynamic innovation portfolios
- Strike the right balance between ideation and execution of innovation management
- Identify pitfalls on the journey of innovation
- Measure the effects of innovation on turnover and market share

Chapter 1 Innovation classification: Digital innovation has a broader spectrum with hybrid nature including incremental innovation, evolutionary innovation, and radical innovation; hard innovations such as products/service innovation, business model or process innovation, and soft innovations such as leadership innovation, communication innovation, and culture innovation. The gap between incremental and radical innovation is huge both in terms of outcomes if successful and on how to approach.

Chapter 2 Innovation principles: Digital brings both unprecedented opportunities and risks to the businesses today. Every innovation-the creative pursuit has the risk of it. You're accepting risk for potential reward. Therefore, it is important to set principles for managing innovation and handling risk in a structural way. The principles and guidelines help to further frame processes, measures, and control.

Chapter 3 Digital innovators: Creativity is a high level of thinking and intelligence. Intelligence is the quick and clear perception of any situation, plus ability to adjust to any circumstances. It is contextual and multidimensional. Digital innovators present leadership skills, master creative communication, understand what is wrong with the status quo, have the good sense and sound judgment to attract and surround themselves with the right people, and work collaboratively to do more with innovation.

Chapter 4 Connecting innovation dots: Creativity is infused with an inner cohesion and comes from a vision of uniqueness. Creativity is simply about connecting the dots. Creativity needs a problem, and a creative person needs a purpose. The difference between innovation and creativity is implementation. Innovation is to reinvent business, but not to reinvent the wheels. Innovation is about reinventing the business direction or purpose, which defines strategy, profitability and relevance at any given time. Innovation allows one to stand out and above the rest.

Chapter 5 Digital innovation next practices: Digital innovation has a broader spectrum with hybrid nature; it is the incremental -substantial- radical innovation continuum. It is hard to think of any innovation as not a hybrid, a combination of something old with something new or a number of new things. Probably, the more hybrid, the more familiar things are combined, the less likely is any disruption, although all innovations are disruptive of something or some behavior to some degree. The innovation leaders need to be skillful in managing complexity and dynamic of innovation portfolio effectively.

Chapter 6 Innovation paradox: Innovation is to transform the novel ideas and achieve their business value. Innovation is not just about ideas or exchanging ideas, based on most of the innovation models, idea creation is only one step of the innovation process. Therefore, in a basic view, innovation is a process and every process needs to be managed. The paradox is that all creative activities are subversive in questioning the status quo. Setting rules and goals for creativity goes against the very nature of creativity and thus inventiveness and innovation. It's critical to strike the right balance between ideation and execution part of the innovation process and management.

Chapter 7 Innovation gaps and pitfalls: Innovation fails because, there are too many disconnects that occur between the birth of a vision/concept and the process of turning it into a reality. Innovation fails because businesses lack cognitive ability to think alternatives. The reasons why failure occurs vary widely. It is no wonder why many leaders are reluctant to act on bold ideas with good business potential due to the high likelihood of failure.

Chapter 8 Innovation measurement: The impact of innovations on enterprise performance ranges from effects on turnover and market share to changes in productivity and efficiency. The problem is often that the initiative is not well defined. Without well-defined goals, you won't have the effective plan and enough time to generate results. So, it is difficult to measure the impact without taking the time to generate impact.

"Innovation is the specific instrument of entrepreneurship...the act that endows resources with a new capacity to create wealth." — Peter F. Drucker

CHAPTER 1

Innovation Classification

The innovation classification is not just based on the required investments, or on the potential market, but on its evolution abilities.

Figure 3 Innovation Classification

For many, innovation is serendipity, for others, it is a buzzword, and it has many definitions. One of the good definitions of innovation is, "intentional novelty bringing sustainable benefit." Innovation is a theme studied in several fields from social applied sciences (like business administration) to engineering. In this way, there's a vast terminology (types of innovation) in what some researchers call incremental (improvement, continuous, modular, component, etc.) and others call radical (breakthrough, disruptive, system, paradigmatic) innovation.

For a business, innovation is 'anything that is new to you.' Any product, process or offering which brings "newness" in its application and results in a measurable value addition may be termed as innovation. Innovation can also be defined based on the differences in non-innovative thinking and work: "High demands and desire and energy for
(1) particularly important and significant added value
(2) for exceptionally strong and utopian solutions
(3) for the realization or prototyping of difficult, unlikely appearing and very challenging solutions.

The innovation classification is based on the position of the concept in the evolution tree. Generally speaking, one small innovation needs fewer resources compared to big innovation (but it's not absolute). Not only time and money but also how to persuade the decision makers to let the idea through stage-gate, mostly because of the level of uncertainty and pertinent risk. This is an important issue to know when categorizing ideas as big/medium/small innovation. Analogically, the innovation classification is based on the position of the concept in the evolution tree: An innovation would be like a big branch, enhancement is like a small branch, the application is like a leaf. We understand with this image that more radical innovation should support other innovation /enhancement/application while enhancement could support only other enhancements or applications. The classification is not based on the required investments, or on the potential market, but on its evolution abilities.

Radical innovation brings something that did not exist before at all, by creating or gathering technologies or processes, in order to bring new steps which can open to other innovations and enhancement. The radical innovation creates a chain of innovation, meaning it necessarily leads to new innovations and enhancements. Enhancement gathers existing processes and technologies to solve a precise problem. It cannot lead to other enhancement except for itself. What happens is that there's not a ruler or scale that say how much an innovation is incremental (small) or radical (big)! Either an innovation is small (incremental) or big (radical), it can still be called innovation, because both are important types of innovation.

Innovation is a question of ambition, and imagination, not a question of investment only. Without ideas that break the mind walls, any innovation department and all its processes and investments will innovate in nothing. Either an innovation is small (incremental) or big (radical), it can still be called innovation because both are important types of innovation. A company should invest part its money in each one of these types to diversify the risks and manage a balanced innovation portfolio. While a radical innovation doesn't appear on the horizon, incremental innovations are the continuous journey, it is fundamental to improve products, services, and processes to compete in today's dynamic market. Innovation is about having new knowledge and new processes. Innovation is the specific phenomenon and strategic imperative of the knowledge-based economy. Innovation is about too much knowledge in terms of too many good creative ideas, and too little available resources. Innovation is about prioritization - a system that can "smell" the right idea at the right time and place. And innovation is an important component of the business strategy.

1 The Breakthrough Innovation

**Innovation means something new and valuable.
Innovation is relative and has a context.**

Innovation has different flavors and also has various
definitions as well. Generally speaking, innovation is how
to transform the novel ideas into products and services to
achieve their business value. Innovation has different types
and can be categorized in a different way: Radical
innovation or breakthrough innovation; evolutionary
innovation or incremental innovation; hard innovation or
soft innovation. Breakthrough innovation changes how
things are being created, it is a revolution, something new
that disrupts or replaces something else. What are the pros
and cons of breakthrough innovation, and how to manage it
effectively?

- **Breakthrough Innovation is better with greater
  ROI but with much greater risk:** Incremental can
  be as rewarding as the initial breakthrough,
  especially if the incremental innovation is based on
  a breakthrough technology you increase and create
  value. Research identifies the projects that
  ultimately break new ground frequently are fraught
  with uncertainty on many dimensions: Technical,
  market, resource and organizational uncertainties
  abound. This requires them to be managed with a
  whole different approach: processes that are fine-
  tuned to deal with uncertainty but not stomp it out

immediately; metrics that take uncertainty into account; team members that thrive in conditions of ambiguity, and a culture that is dramatically different from the operational excellence orientation that dominates incremental innovation.

- **Breakthrough Innovation is disruptive and will change your organization in many fields:** You need new technology, new processes, new customers, new knowledge, may be a new business model. All that makes them very risky but on the other hand, you will get very great chances and opportunities for new product lines, platforms etc. They will need them in strategic long-range view. There are cases where incremental innovation has resulted in breakthrough impacts. Perhaps the terms should be used in the context of the desired outcomes rather than as process descriptions or technological developments. Breakthrough implies a distinction in innovative solution at any type of innovation. Breakthrough Innovation is a radical new approach that leaves competitions behind in some way. Breakthrough innovation is out of the box thinking while incremental innovation is still inside the box thinking. Incremental innovation is what is used after the breakthrough to "touch" things up a bit. It is much more predictable, often the result of optimization efforts on the product or process.

- **Breakthrough Innovation is 'new to the world':** It is 'anything new to businesses or purists want to

call it as 'new to the world'; something that no one else has done before; really original. Breakthrough innovation might be thought of as an initial innovation in an area, possibly the one shows that innovation is possible or gives a new route. Perhaps it is a major discovery regarding the area. It is generally not so predictable and may require a lot of luck, or advanced knowledge in one or more areas to accomplish. Breakthrough innovation is in the future with no necessary continuity with the past. Breakthroughs have four key components:
(1) Takes Advantage of Emerging Trends.
(2) Provides for Basic Human Needs.
(3) Uses Simple Business Models.
(4) Build Barriers to Entry - by combining different choices about target markets, offerings, channels, and partnerships, breakthroughs are not easily achieved.

When a company "thinks differently," implements new ways to solve problems, and then you have innovation. Innovation means something new and valuable. Innovation is relative and has a context. The key to innovation success is just as simple, innovation is nothing without exploration and exploitation.

2 "Incremental" Innovation

You cannot "disrupt" without incremental innovation being part of the process.

Innovation is in the eye of the beholder – hopefully, a customer. The only test for whether it is or is not an innovation is whether it makes any difference to a dimension that is valued by whoever has a stake in your offering, it is best if that happens to be the customer. If the innovation is meeting a need, expressed or otherwise, it is an innovation. Adding value is the characteristics of an innovation. Too often, companies announce ambitious "breakthrough" initiatives, only to see them rapidly folding back to "business-as-usual." This is a problem and this problem must be confronted. The nature of innovation varies depending on whether you are within a paradigm in your industry or the context in your environment, requires crossing paradigm boundaries. A "tweak" that adds mutual value to both the customer and the provider can still be an innovation, the difference being a matter of degree. Incremental innovation has become the value that the customer expects you to provide if you are to remain a sustainable supporting innovation, the unexpected disruption that can re-structure the competitive landscape. Any incremental improvement of a product that allows the company to increase sales, revenue, profit margins, or market share, etc, is innovation.

- **Build innovation capability**: Breakthroughs/Transformational Innovations are not something everyone can accomplish. You have to systematically develop the capability to execute it successfully, and that is something you do not accomplish overnight. You can have a vision, but that does not mean you can do it right away. On the roadmap for developing the capability to successfully and perhaps continuously deliver transformational innovations, there are a number of incremental opportunities that are also innovation. The ambitious, radical, market-changing innovations are specifically enabled by complete, systems-level specifications of all the relevant valued product or service interactions currently and potentially tied to the targeted product or service. Incremental design requirements most often produce incremental innovation results. Such evolutionary efforts often produce quite respectable financial results. On the other hand, when an individual or organization claims they are investing in and managing an ambitious innovation project and then immediately cripples the breadth of possible innovations by prioritizing design requirements down to only the "most important one." Incremental design requirements most often produce incremental innovation results and relatively limit financial returns, for that matter. Sometimes "logically" focused on only the most important current problems with the product or service are exactly the reason why innovation projects are often found to be risky and fail. Hence, it is crucial to building innovation capability for the business's long-term prosperity.

- **Improvement-innovation continuum:** Incremental innovation is actually a critical part of breakthrough or disruptive innovation. Innovation is not a singular idea or event, as a key part of the innovation is the behavioral changes that occur as the idea is adopted by a user group. Most people are aware of the classic "S" curve adoption patterns of innovation, which is a time-based model. Things that drive adoption up the S-curve are the incremental innovations that continue to improve the value propositions, decrease costs and expand supporting market infrastructure, which in turn drive expanded adoption. Very few, if any, disruptive concepts emerge directly into the mainstream. The disruptive impact is a cumulative effect of continuous incremental innovation of the initial idea over time. You cannot "disrupt" without incremental innovation being part of the process.

- **The solution to the "incremental vs. breakthrough innovation dilemma' is portfolio management**: The realities of corporate life don't allow companies to spend all their resources on radical, and thus intrinsically more risky innovation. It's generally believed that companies should have a balanced portfolio of innovation projects composed of ~70% of "incremental" innovations, ~20% of "adjacent" and ~10% of "radical/breakthrough innovation" Obviously, the precise ratio is dependent on the age/size of the company. The "three-horizon strategy" is the name for this approach. Currently accepted corporate management practice most often begins innovation projects by prioritizing the many possible areas of improvements in the customer (or another stakeholder) experience and then focusing on only those "most important" areas which the design team estimates will have the greatest ROI. This common management practice tends to automatically limit each design cycle to small evolutionary/incremental design improvements specifically because the design team is focused on innovations in only one part of the total system of valued product interactions. The team's opportunity to innovate is limited from the start of the project. In direct contrast, revolutionary design innovations most often require design teams to attend to the total system of all valued product interactions and related opportunities to systematically create new design features that efficiently enable new value across wide ranges of current and new product interactions. Such tour de force efforts and results are what most of the businesses get excited about when working on "innovation" projects.

Innovation comes in many flavors and there are many opportunities in an enterprise to do so. Incremental innovation is a quantitative progress and radical innovation is a transformational leapfrog. A healthy innovation portfolio needs to have both in order to reach innovation horizon with the optimal speed at the right time.

3 Open Innovation

The very nature of open innovation is to take advantage of all sources of creativity in a more open way and make a leap of innovation management to the next level.

Innovation has different types: Radical innovation/breakthrough innovation; evolutionary innovation or incremental innovation; innovation also has different flavors: Open innovation or closed innovation. Open innovation = innovation whereby a company uses the ideas, sources or help of people outside the company. These people are normally business partners, customers or crowd-sourcing consultants. Closed innovation = Innovation whereby a company uses their internal R&D or talent across-company for managing innovation lifecycle.

- **The value of open innovation is increasing:** Open innovation not only lies in an industry that is rapidly growing and market participants are small and fragmented; but also in the mature sectors or traditional companies that only innovation can rejuvenate their business via breaking down the bureaucratic culture. The smaller players can gain economies of scale through collaboration. The paradigm shifts when these clusters morph into larger entities that have sufficiently large internal resources to develop closed innovation. The well-established large organizations can also benefit from open innovation to fully involve with their partners or customers and take outside-in perspectives. The challenge to innovate (either open or closed way) is a problem when these entities transform into bureaucratic corporations!

- **The company has to determine what can be open and what can be closed:** "Openness" and "closeness" are decisions relate to the architecture of new products generation model. But, different from another "open" propositions, like open source and creative commons, open innovation doesn't have the assumption of total information openness. There is no obligation of abdicating of property in the open innovation model. Open innovation uses all the information sources available in developing a robust innovation pipeline to improve innovation management effectiveness. Open innovation makes the pie of creative ideas grow bigger. Innovations simply benefit from being developed in, and subsequently commercialized in a more open ecosystem. There is more flow of creative ideas, the more is happening, the pie gets bigger. Now the debate seems to be in which conditions this more open cooperative ecosystem paradigm can never ever work for all eternity; or whether it is simply a matter of getting used to these forms of working and commercializing value in the digital era with the new characteristics of hyper-connectivity and convergence.

- **Open innovation is a new business paradigm:** Open innovation is about monetizing the value of specific technologies, which would otherwise, if remain closed, have little or no value. At least to the extent big corporations are involved. The greater good of humanity, of course, maybe a side product. It is for finding better pastures off the fence for innovation experiment. Though, open innovations are not as open as one may think; it requires participants to seek legal licenses with limitations and restrictions that benefit the originator of the innovation. Either open or closed way, businesses are hunting for revolutionary, path-breaking, disruptive or substantially incremental technologies, not just in "me too" or marginally incremental innovations only.

Digitalization stipulates companies working together in a hyper-connected and continuously converging environment that provides structural analysis and a certain extent of serendipity. The evolution of innovation only exists in these more open environments that create insights, take advantage of all sources of creativity in a more open way and make a leap of innovation management to the next level.

4 Business Model Innovation

The mindset, vision, competency, capability, culture and marketing opportunity are all great starting point for business model innovation.

A business model is a multi-level, zoom-able schema of how a business or an organization creates, delivers, and captures value for stakeholders: Customers, businesses, investors, or society. A business model is the set of features of a business that keep it in business. If you have a strong business model, you have a set of value-generating skills that match customer need and are difficult to copy, at least in the short term. Often this is a strong relationship between differentiation and cost. A strong business model is difficult to copy; it is differentiated in the marketplace. The business model design is one of the critical types of innovation that enable business growth and compete for the future. However, most of such effort fails to achieve the expected result.

- **The starting point of business model innovation reflects one's state of mind:** A business model is "why this business works." If you can't answer that in a few words, you probably don't have a viable business! The business model defines customers, needs and solutions as well as competitive advantage. Ideally, a business balances its activities and resources in such a way, that it can be successful at both creating new forms of value and delivering and capturing from its existing forms. In this way, a strong business is wired to purposefully and strategically change its business model. The starting point of business model innovation reflects one's state of mind, so when you begin to design the model, you have to, as a business leader, be very clear what you are and how you want to approach the market. That would determine your starting points. When you define the direction in which you want your business to travel, you need to ask a series of definitive questions. The strategizing process should start with understanding the style of the leadership, what the leadership preaches, and what it actually promotes. The style of the leadership is imbued with mind-maps, with past situations, and with future hopes that in an unstable form - condition the state-of-mind. Your state of mind (mood/outlook) can vary massively throughout this process! Your state of mind can vary from day to day! Anyone's starting point reflects one's state of mind!

- **Competencies /dream /vision/culture**: You need to identify core competencies and critical capabilities as well as where the future will be for the business entity model design (expansion/consolidation/emerging field trend and predictions). Starting the business model based on the technologic vision and on the mega-trends is to be able to build the core competencies and the critical capabilities early enough to catch the wave before its crest breaks. The core competencies and the critical capabilities are probably what the senior management should focus on. Look at whom and what you have to work with before you define the expected outcomes! Please note the former fixates the intangible resources, while the latter focuses on the tangible resources. In a business environment that is driven by change, it enables senior management to keep evolving their core competencies and the critical capabilities so as to keep their enterprise ahead of the crest of the wave. Culture eats innovation for lunch. No matter where you start your business model from (customer needs, technological leaps, market gaps, etc.), it will mean very little unless you also simultaneously build a culture that can execute, which takes two major things, hiring and promoting people with digital mindset, and designing internal processes that promote the right behaviors and culture. After eating strategy for breakfast, now culture is hunting innovation for lunch. Hence, strategy, structure, and culture must be developed in tandem with real sustainability.

- **Examine the market to describe the opportunity**: Is the market growing? How large is it today and what are projections for the future? How many suppliers are there, and are they dominant in market share? Are current suppliers able to supply the anticipated future growth? What is the cost of entry? Is this a market that competes on price, quality, innovation, service, and other factors? What is the cost point to be competitive? What is your strategic advantage? What percentage of that market do you expect to capture over what period of time? Why would someone prefer to buy from you? What are your vision and mission? The starting point for a business model differs based on the objectives and nature of an organization as well. But just following trends in your own sector is a sure way to lose! Trends are just a means to end- successful (and profitable) innovations. It's all about foreseeing and applying trends, that's where you win the competitive edge. Understanding customer insights and purchasing trends is the key to any future business/marketing strategies. However, creating trends is about anticipating direction.

The mindset, vision, competency, capability, culture and marketing opportunity are all great starting point for business model innovation. The senior management frame is important in complicated systems subject to biases and the forces of change. Business models can be holistically evolved through feedback loops and probes, subjectively and objective evolved, refined, changed, the process measured and then repeated.

5 Design-Driven Innovation

The purpose of Design-Driven Innovation is to Delight Customer.

Nowadays, innovation has many flavors, from open innovation to systematic approach; from customer-centricity to the technology breakthrough. Here comes design-driven innovation.

- **Design becomes the strategic business driver at higher level maturity:** As an organization's maturity about design increased, design moves from a superficial afterthought (branding a design) to competitive advantage (branding through design). Very few companies can arrive at the top of the design maturity ladder. Design becomes a strategic business driver equal to business and technology. Design thought has stages of maturity: From design-by-default, where design just happens and design is dictated by status quo policies, procedures, tools, and old mindsets, to design –by-practice, where design becomes the key ingredient of innovation strategy, and design-driven innovation has been supported by cohesive business capability, well-tuned business processes and high-skilled talent teams with open mind working at creative business environment.

- **Design vs. Art**: Design and art are different, the art looks inward; the design looks outward. Good art is much more than self-expression; good design is much more than decoration. It is about composition and designers seek a different kind of inspiration. Tools for design are user personas, scenarios, and storyboards. Design can be art, but too often is not. The art enters the project at the beginning - as the concept (often arrived at by a brainstorming session). One more difference between art and design: Designers test; artists don't. The problems begin when designers forget users and start considering themselves artists. Such confusion of art with the design is what gets designers confined to the role of the very most superficial decoration. Although design concerns itself with aesthetics, design is not superficial decoration.

- **Design-driven Innovation needs to have strong communication between design teams and management:** The open-mindedness fostered by a brainstorming session would be a good place to start communicating this to management. They really need to get together during a brainstorm session. And in talking about design thinking, management gets buy-in. The winning chips represent actual commitment -- of people, of time, of funding -- from the players get cashed in by the winner, who becomes the project champion. The construct of a design-driven innovation game allows the open-mindedness brainstorming. But the constructs within the game bring this down to earth and anchor it in pragmatics and commitment. Essentially, it takes "change management in a box" with some assembly required.

In short, very little emphasis or consideration is placed on design methodologies cross-industries. The design is largely considered a byproduct of solid engineering discipline. The design takes planning and fine-tuning that must take place to deliver the product. This part is more like engineering than art, but if done correctly, the final product retains that core kernel of art. It is not spontaneous. But do you really think the masters didn't plan their masterpieces? For design thinking and design-driven innovation to reach its full potential, organizations need to have a well-planned innovation strategy, fined tuned processes, skilled talent, and disciplined approach.

6 Management Innovation

Management innovation has both hard elements such as process and metrics; and soft elements such as communication and culture.

Innovation is the light every organization is pursuing, however, from the variety of industry studies; most companies do renovating instead of innovating; what're the underlying problems? Does that mean management innovation is perhaps the new angle to see through innovation management, as management innovation changes the way managers do what they do to improve organizational performance, where innovation is one of many management practices, but the critical one.

- **Problem-solving mindset**: Both management innovation and innovation management start with mind shift. Rather than see innovation as a goal, it would be best to see it as a set of tools to be used to address specific business issues in running a healthy and growing business. Many companies set out to innovate before defining the role that innovation will play in the business as a whole and where it fits into the overall strategy. It also needs to align innovation strategy with key ingredients of management innovation, such as the development of an innovative culture or business eco-system, which requires grounding in values, behaviors, systems and artifacts as well as collaboration with key stakeholders. The other thing is that organizations can't afford the risk of not engaging in disruptive innovation. So, the point is not to denigrate incremental improvements in favor of "breakthroughs," but how to achieve both. In ambidextrous organizations, this is achieved by careful innovation portfolio management. So, without management innovation, companies tend to renovate rather than innovate, move very slow for making innovations in other areas such as, culture, technology, service etc.

- **The management styles/tradition and the corporate culture play an essential role:** The management innovation includes multiple elements such as communication innovation, culture innovation, process innovation, etc, management innovation can be very powerful, yet, and it really comes with personal risks as you get close to the "core of power and control." To achieve that, the right atmosphere should be created and maintained. The main issues of such atmosphere are:

(1) **No fear**: When fear is present, brilliant ideas wait for better time or just diminish.

(2) **Reward innovators**: The person that brought the brilliant idea is not responsible for persuading the management of why is it a good idea, because, most brilliant minds in innovation are not strong in organizational politics. The organization should do that task and credit the person thought of the brilliant idea.

(3) **The support process**: The innovation only begins with brilliant ideas. The organization should develop the idea to the point that it is a product or service.

- **Management innovation takes cross-functional collaboration, which is imperative for innovation management:** The biggest problem is that the entire company is structured and organized to produce what they currently produce and it is staffed primarily to keep the current business humming. It is very difficult to have "Big Innovation" efforts vie for the same resources needed for implementation, especially when they lack the hard, historical metrics that companies are used for their decision-making. More specifically, due to the fear of failure, most companies renovate rather than innovate because of a lack of alignment between IT, Marketing, and the C-Suite. The problem is that in a lot of organizations, many departments think and operate independently of each other. In order to better understand a potential innovation, you require brainpower from all the right areas of expertise to contribute their thoughts on that innovation's feasibility. Once this process takes place, or the management innovation tone is well set, the talent in charge have brought in with this new strategy, and with the collective knowledge of the company, it's likely you can accelerate the implementation of the ideas as well.

- **Management innovation means to accelerate innovation at the multitude of levels:** It's important to create the space for dialogue and debate about why it is important for their organization, developing a common understanding of it, creating the necessity and motivation for it. Enterprises that are able to successfully innovate at a breakthrough level can increase the likelihood that they will dominate and prosper in new markets that they create. Enterprises that restrict themselves to incremental innovation, on the other hand, risk unknowingly entering a vicious cycle in which they lag ever farther behind. There are two dominant obstacles that stand in the way of driving higher returns from innovation. A first challenge is a conservative approach itself, focusing on individual line extension renovation rather than developing a broader portfolio. Renovation can limit innovation to small incremental improvements and fail to result in significant step changes and revenue opportunities.

Innovation is an exploration, production, adoption, assimilation, and exploitation of value-added novelty in business, economic and social spheres. Management innovation and innovation management will go hand in hand, mutually enforce each other to achieve the full business values of innovation.

7 Culture Innovation

Hire Mindset, build capability, and harness creativity.

People are the most invaluable asset in business, at the age of digital, it is, even more, true than ever. Talented employees are treated as human capital needs to be well invested to unleash the boundless potential, not just human resources counted as a cost. HR needs to transform itself from an administration function and gatekeeper to change agent, capital investor and innovator in order to build a creative digital working environment and catalyze the organizational level of digital transformation. However, how do you, as leaders, involve all people in creative thinking and actions? And how can you help improve the harvest of the creative seeds?

- **There's no one size global solution- but there are certainly significant core principles and common practices to experiment and experience:**
Creativity has a language, but it is altogether different from the one found in the traditional business environment. Generally speaking, you must allow room for failure, for tangents, for being "different." Creativity is a long-term endeavor. It must be cultivated, but most businesses measure success at the end of every growth cycle. Most businesses value mono-culture, homogeneous leadership; reward mediocre, and overly encourage "the spirit of animal," which often motivate negative workforce competition. There are core principles in building a creative working environment:
- Allow autonomy; let people choose how and on what they work
- Create a safe environment for learning from failure
- Provide intellectual challenge and help people make progress
- Foster integrity, trust, and transparency
- Encourage curiosity and a growth mindset
- Help people feel more comfortable with chaos, uncertainty, and ambiguity

- Encourage people to question the status quo and think independently
- Create an environment that encourages dissent and candor
- Allow time for play and experimentation
- Establish clear, shared innovation goals

- **The second half of the creativity equation belongs to the team member:** People can be creative in the way they think or act or even in working on projects that excite them. And that's good, but the bottom line can't be ignored and as a business leader, you do need to show some ROI over time. Additionally, some people are creative by nature and thrive in a free-flowing environment and some of their ideas may bear fruit; the others value order and structure and are not creative by nature; it takes two-way effort – the management's empowerment and the employees' attitude and aptitude. Creativity is individual. It is, by nature, unique to each person. There is no template which you can apply and suddenly have a creative workforce. It must be done slowly, patiently, and individually; otherwise, that seems like scattering a bunch of seeds on the wind and seeing which ones germinate. It depends on the nature of the company, its people, and ambitions.

- **Customer-centric solutions often come from the floor and not the ceiling:** The talent management gurus brainstorm the idea of 'productive friction' as a way of encouraging and instilling a creative and innovative environment. At industrial silos, people are treated as resources and cost, and most works are operational in nature; however, digital breaks down such silo thinking, creativity can make many operational works more effective, doing the right things, rather than just doing the things right. Every staff should strive to become a customer evangelist or a culture champion; especially there are all different types of work activities, roles, industries, require great deals of creativity.

- **The best way to foster creativity is to help people communicate in a way that instills confidence, not fear**: Nowadays, most of the traditional organizations are "busy-ness" to focus only on transactional effort, the trying-to-get-a-leg-up atmosphere in many companies squashes any tiny seed of creativity. As businesses get more cut-throat in the hyper-connected digital working environment, this puts stress on the labor force that is not conducive to more creative and experimental thinking. That is why so many companies won't do it. If you want to make a "creative culture" in the company. you need to give talent:
  - A "place" to expand their knowledge
  - A chance to apply their ideas
  - Recognition for their idea
  - No embedding behavior or hidden rules in the office
  - And make a collaboration culture in the company

- **Developing a culture of creativity is, by nature, a cultural change:** In the workplace where creativity is not always valued, to involve everyone in creativity and to provide a focused approach to real business problems, companies can benefit from taking a structured approach to developing a culture of creativity. Organizations should empower innovators and encourage multidimensional thinking such as, dynamic thinking, independent thinking, systems thinking, complexity thinking and creative thinking. Such "thought-provoking" innovative talent continuously invests in adopting and adapting habits of mind that allow them to think and respond to challenges critically and creatively. In doing so they are able to think holistically about themselves, their team, their relationships with others, the organizations to which they belong, their work, and the environments in which they live and work. They are truth-seeking, willing to change their views and are accountable for their actions. Furthermore, they are robust and judicious in pushing down barriers to achieve the best possible effects. If all talent staff can learn to think like this, and then, we'll be better equipped to adapt and thrive in the ever-changing, increasingly unpredictable and uncertain digital world in which we live.

Great leaders are creative themselves, who can inspire, provoke, empower and enable talent growth, provide direction when needed, give others time, space, and freedom to create. They create a suitable and hybrid (physical + virtual) environment for creativity, stimulate and measure the originality and creativity, focus on cross-generational digital professionals who bring new ideas. And the system of curricula (training, performance management) should be revised to expand the skills on this attitude.

8 The Collective Creativity

The exercise of blending people's problem-solving abilities to produce the desired outcome is a worthwhile thing to do.

There are still full of serendipity in creativity: How many forms of creativity are there? How are they different? How are they similar? Isn't what makes them similar or different, also what makes them creativity? Individual creativity is absolutely critical, but how to harness the collective creativity?

- **Creativity can manifest in a collective environment:** While the individual contributions provide the 'building block' of creativity, it is the collective consensus on what to do with them is exciting. The purpose of pursuing collective creativity is based on:

  - the intent of the event was to develop a tangible result that did not currently exist.

-the nature of the result was deliberately expressive and improvised.

-the interactions between participants were not premeditated or contrived.

- the resulting 'product' was more than any one individual was capable of achieving.

-the result was not something that anyone participant could have conceived Independently.

- **The exercise of blending people's problem-solving abilities to produce the desired outcome is a worthwhile thing to do:** It is not just a mere accumulation of the creative inputs of those involved. It is also not only synchronizing of their individual inputs to make something that no one individual would achieve. It is more than that. It has its own dynamic that is in a state of constant flux. It (on occasions) builds up a momentum that draws creative contributions from the participants that they did not previously conceive or understood what they were capable of. Whether creativity can be collective is clear and flows from what seems like an expansive, generous, creative mind, and illustrates the 'Third Alternative' synergistic result Steven Covey, the author of "7 Habits of Highly Effective People," refers to when the final result is bigger than the intentions of the individuals involved. It is indeed creative to push, invite, allow, and accept ideas from a group to reach a final result not originally predicted because it requires the openness to create a new idea and allow it to form fully.

- **The collective creativity depends on varying factors**: Being creative is the kind to "think outside the box" for ideas and solutions. But the creative spark does not always originate solely in the individual. In that manner, you could say there is more collective creativity happening everywhere than many realize because it is really hard for some people to see outside of their own box. Also, the group of people does not always make creativity blossom. You can get a diverse group of people together in one room and still not have "creativity" if the participating individuals are not particularly creative. What matters is how creative the individuals are. Hence, the collective creativity depends on varying factors, because the teams perhaps have different intents (destructive vs. constructive), different processes (enforcement vs. collaboration), different participants (compliant vs. creative), different outcomes (disharmony vs. harmony) and different philosophies (selfishness vs. selflessness).

Creativity has many forms and manifestations. Take the standpoint that creativity has its starting point within an individual. Once we take into consideration the influences around this person (environment, culture, principles, etc.), their creativity will manifest in different forms. From its starting within an individual to the point where it becomes external to them (visually, aurally, tactile, etc.), it cannot be identical from one person to another. By manifesting creativity from an individual endeavor to a team activity and a collective effort, the horizon of creativity is expanded, it converges with the concept of innovation that is the management discipline to transform innate ideas and achieve their business value.

9 A Digital Innovation Ecosystem

An innovation ecosystem is a systematic innovation methodological environment or a sort of innovation philosophy.

Innovation is the change to tackle the complexities of business dynamic, but within itself, it needs to change as well. There is a paradigm shift that is taking place in generating innovation and building a scalable innovation environment or innovation ecosystem.

- **An innovation ecosystem should fully cover a wide enough direction:** For example, cost optimization, waste reduction, quality improvement, capability orchestration, problem-solving etc. When the designed objects' scale becomes bigger, it involves more and more aspects widely, so the businesses need innovation silver lining from specific tools rising to an overall problem-solving system environment.

- **"Systemic" vs. "Systematic" Innovation**: "Systemic" relates to "from within" or the genes of the organization. It ties to cultural and leadership aspects (soft factors) of innovation where "systematic" relates to capacities of hard methodologies, practices, and tools. Hence, there is a need for innovative methods or tools around, but they neither create nor replace the culture, leadership, commitment, reward system etc, in building systemic innovation.

- **There are many components in an effective innovation environment or ecosystem:** Each component by itself may not cause a good environment, but collectively, they can and weave an innovation ecosystem such as innovation leadership, innovation culture, innovation capability, practices, tools, recognition system measurements, risk approach. Innovation ecosystem or the methodological environment should cover the whole innovation process, from processes in managing ideas or idea handling systems to idea implementation and promotion. That's why it is a set of means including methods that cover the process from the problem's choice till commercialization.

- **An innovation ecosystem is a systematic innovation methodological environment or a sort of "professional philosophy" for innovation**: An enriched innovation ecosystem enables systematic innovation management. It starts with innovation strategy defines "What does the organization innovate" or "where should it innovate" to support the overall strategy. The strategy is tightly connected to the business model and provides the context for the innovation. The organizational content is the innovation capability which is how the organization innovates.

- **Variety, complexity, diversification, and collaboration are the characteristics of the digital innovation ecosystem:** Organizations can no longer rely on a single individual or team to drive innovation. This is largely due to the fact that innovating in today's digital world has become increasingly complex in nature. Innovation needs to lay out different structures, thinking and solutions to allow this to develop in its potential where organizations are combining all that is available to them in imaginative and advantageous ways. This is why so many leaders have begun using collaborative methodologies as infrastructures to orchestrate their organization's talent and bring out their collective best thinking to accelerate innovation and optimize their solution forming capabilities.

The business competitiveness is gated by innovation, and their innovation is gated by their ability to "systematize" innovation as opposed to relying on sporadic talent. Therefore, the innovation ecosystem is for the long-term and more of a catalyst for scaling up innovation.

CHAPTER 2

Innovation Principles

Being innovative is more important than any specific innovation. Innovativeness is a way of thinking.

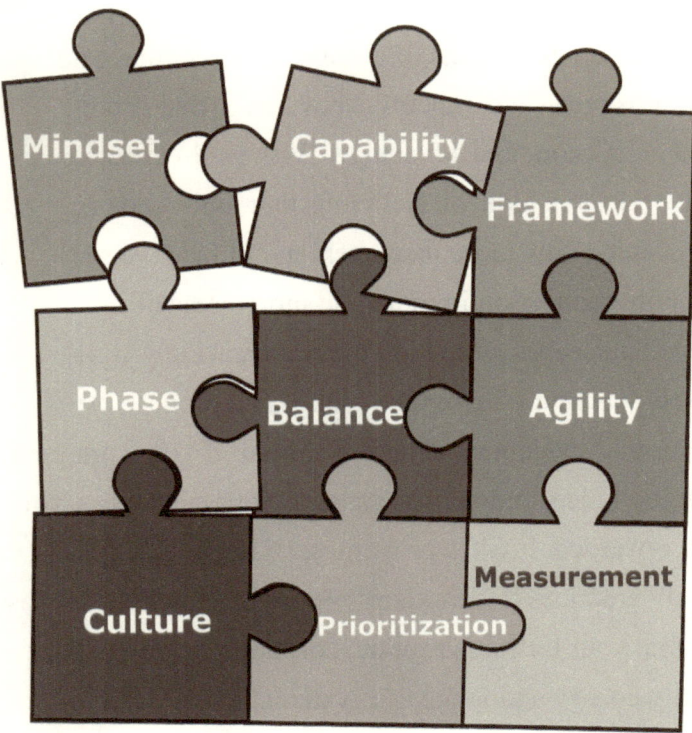

Figure 4 Innovation Principles

We're approaching the digital world with complexity, hyperconnectivity, and the highest level of education ever, and as a result, more people are competing in an increasingly competitive global arena. Joseph Alois Schumpeter was an Austrian-born American economist and one of the 20th century's greatest intellectuals. One of the most common themes in Schumpeter's theories was the role of innovation, and entrepreneurship in economic growth, well-known as "Creative disruption." The classic Schumpeterian definitions of innovation stress that true innovations create a competitive advantage that is not limited to an economic advantage. With well-educated digital workforce today, it's obvious that innovation is being pursued now more than ever, and in fact, we see much more innovation in more and more areas of the business landscapes as a result of an increasingly well-educated population across the globe. The purpose of Innovation Management is just so simple: If you work hard, have a good idea, and deliver value to your customers, you will be rewarded. It takes principles, strategy, discipline, and daily practices to flex your "innovation muscle. " It has to become your business routine, corporate culture to renew creativity energy and it needs a systematic approach to running a balanced innovation portfolio for building innovation strength in your organization continually. Here are nine principles to enforce innovativeness and improve innovation management effectiveness.

#1 Mindset - <u>Being innovative is more important than any specific innovation</u>: Innovativeness is a way of thinking. While the change was often previously discrete, intermittent, and predictable, it is now constant, discontinuous, and unpredictable, so we need to change the way we change. This is where absorptive capacity, dynamic capabilities, learning agility, etc. are needed. We don't really know the future of the industry or the environment, but we prepare ourselves to create it better and compete in it. 'True innovation—opportunities missed by most people." Thomas Edison famously said, because they're "dressed in overalls and look like work." Innovation is the idea brought to market even when other people thought the idea was crazy or too obvious, and later when it leads to success, everyone looks at and says, "I wish I had thought of that!"

#2 Capability - <u>Looking at innovation from the perspective of developing business-wide innovation capabilities</u>: This requires an effective 'innovation system' that is capable of supporting both widespread incremental innovation in products/services and ways of working as well as the rarer 'step-change' innovation in products/services, working methodology, business model, and market positioning.

Innovation has three "**D**"s phases: **D**iscovery of a problem or new idea; **D**esigning a prototype solution and the ultimate **D**elivery of a commercially astute outcome. That the best point of view is to see innovation as a system, capable of delivering organization-wide capability. If you look at all the attempts over the last few decades to create a mutually exclusive and collectively exhaustive typology for innovation, you will soon realize that it is probably not possible given that almost every area of human endeavor is subject to change and thus "innovation." The three classic qualifiers (novelty, value, and implementation) are possible to satisfy in any area, so anything is fair game.

#3 Framework - <u>Build an effective innovation framework to manage innovation in a structural way</u>**:** Innovation Management System includes policies, structure, and program that innovation managers can use to drive innovation. Remove any of the three, you're liable to fail. A defined structure is essential to managing innovation in a corporation, but there's no single structure that will work in every organization. More precisely, you don't structure innovation. You apply principles of approach and vary the resource and tool mix by the ever-changing environment, day to day through the year to year. Trying to use overly rigid structure applies limits to unleash full innovation potential. If the structure is meant in a methodological sense, then the structure is needed. For example, ideas are crucial to an innovation program. You need to make sure, that your company has a steady flow of fresh ideas floating in your innovation pipeline, and, therefore, you need a methodological platform that allows you to do that. Money facilitates innovation, but does not guarantee the result. What you are primarily doing is harvesting ideas that have emerged and are waiting to be picked. The money will increase the willingness of employees to contribute the ideas or improve innovation management system. It doesn't mean though that it will increase the volume of ideas that are available to be collected. However, as processes yielding results, innovation and efficiency can complement and enhance each other, the balance of efficiency and innovation is the most challenging continuity regardless of the emphasis. The process to support the creation of sustainable, systematic innovation can be structured, but innovation per se is like composing a symphony, a lot of planning, but the music will come from the musicians, not the conductor.

#4 Phase - <u>Businesses need to determine where best to focus their innovation activities</u>: From a business perspective, 'anything new to your business' is an effective definition to encourage both large and small ideas and ideas that are new and 'copied with pride' from others. If it brings increased value to the business, then that's what's important, not semantics. Establishing sustained and institutional-level innovation is the goal. Innovation consists of two phases: The creative ideation up front, and then the sharing and implementation downstream when explaining, developing, and selling to sufficiently involve others in adopting and improving upon the "excitement." In other words, the "moment of Eureka" may be very exciting, but hanging on for the long-term adoption and extended use phases may become quickly challenging and exhausting. So, it pays to learn to view innovation matters realistically, and manage innovation phases and processes effectively.

#5 Balance - Successful innovation is finding the bridge between 'push' and 'pull': Businesses and the world are pushed forward by exponential changes and fierce competitions. And commercial innovation implementation may be represented by creating a need for or finding a need for a 'pull.' To build that bridge requires enthusiasm, belief, determination and commitment as well as a good business case. Innovation is not so much a system, although you need to have processes in place, but more a responsive way of working in general. There are breakthrough innovations or radical innovations, evolutionary innovations, and incremental innovations as well. The minimum requirement for innovation is that the product, process, marketing method or organizational method must be new (or significantly improved) to the firm. This includes products, processes, and methods that firms are the first to develop and those that have been adopted by other firms or organizations. "Pushing" only is not efficient to drive innovation, because idea creation scenario takes brainstorming, collaboration, knowledge absorbing and insight capture. Hence, it's important for managers to pull all necessary resource and build a culture of creativity to harvest from sowing the seeds of innovation to making new ideas fruitful.

#6 Agility - 'Innovation Agility' enables people to see and solve problems in flexible and adaptive ways: It is about incorporating entrepreneurial and startup principles, with a focus on reducing risk adversity to add value to the quality of people's lives. This involves thinking systemically because it involves organizational climate, culture, and process changes, simultaneously, within a business ecosystem context. Innovation as the creation and development of new ideas causes meaningful change for customers and the company. This isn't always a new product or service but can also be an improvement in processes, employee satisfaction or the environmental impact. If it makes your customers happier, the firm will eventually also benefit from that!

#7 Culture - Innovation must be part of the organization's DNA - Culture: Instead of creating overly rigid processes, first, it's more practical to create a set of digital innovation principles which are based on collaboration and co-creation. Innovation is not that difficult, but this is not to say that generating great new idea is not hard. Creativity in the "corporate" world has a lot to do with fostering a creative environment. Innovation will happen when people are given free space to be creative without rigid structures and without holding them back. If the environment is all about "you have to cover your back/mistakes," and then all the creativity in the world goes out of the window. If one is in an environment where he or she is allowed to make mistakes and learn from them; then it's great for both, the individual and the company and the creative strength is built at the corporate level. Innovation comes with a risk of failure, usually not well tolerated in risk avoidance mind, protecting the interests of short-term benefit. Therefore, innovators should always have the greater vision in mind and strive to return sustainable development and growth back to the business or society they are working in/for. The benefit is mutual. Innovation can have brand effect as well if the large successful organizations once have established themselves as thought leaders or indeed product innovation leaders often trade on their brand. Innovation is a culture more than anything, and it occurs of its own volition and often on its own timescale.

#8 Prioritization: <u>Setting innovation priorities right significantly improves innovation management effectiveness</u>: Build innovation strength via prioritizing resources, managing risks with a portfolio management approach. Innovation is a disciplined approach to discovering and building opportunities in creating new meaningful sources of value to targeted users. Innovation is the sustainable and scalable way that can be learned and practiced. Building a balanced innovation portfolio is a practical approach to optimizing resource and improving risk intelligence. Because innovation is not all about products and services, it can also be used for cost reductions, process and business model changes and improvement. It is hard to think of any innovation as not a hybrid, a combination of something old with something new or a number of new things. Probably, the more hybrid, the more familiar things are combined, the less likely is any disruption. The realities of corporate life don't allow companies to spend all their resources on radical innovation, and thus, more intrinsically risky innovation. It's generally believed that companies should have a balanced portfolio of innovation projects composed of 70%-80% of "incremental" innovations, 10~20% of "adjacent" and 5~10% of "radical/breakthrough." The precise ratio is dependent on the age/size of the company in some sense, to a particular need, whether individual, group or industry. Innovation is about transforming novel ideas to achieve their business value. Without a profit motive, it doesn't work. Leveraging tailored tools in effective innovation management is important to improve its success rate. The organizations with the healthy innovation appetites and systematic approach would enjoy the balanced innovation portfolio with well-mixed radical innovation and incremental innovation projects.

#9 Measurement - Select a right set of innovation KPIs and measure them in the right way. There is no best practice solution which fits all cases. Normally organizations look for KPIs measuring business results generated by innovation efforts. But it takes quite some time for a new innovation drive to produce those measures. One of the solutions is to define process KPIs, which demonstrate the growing capability of the organization to deliver more innovation with business impact in the future.

You choose those KPIs by deciding which are seen as critical to making progress in order to deliver more innovations. The fewer the better, but they have to be credible and relevant also in the eyes of the stakeholders. For example, culture is a perfect (sometimes it gets even too complicated) metric system to measure the impact of innovation on the business in order to unleash more successful, transformational innovations.

Innovation is the development of a new combination of available resources, in a way that solves problems of others in a more suitable way. Using the principles of adaptive innovation, one starts with the amount or quality of time itself translated into major societal need. From a business perspective, shaping innovative mindsets, building innovation capability, and cultivating innovation agility are all crucial in making innovation management more practical than just serendipity.

1 Five Guidelines to Catalyze Digital Innovation

Businesses need the well-defined set of guidelines and rules for managing innovation risks in a structural way.

Innovation is the light every forward-looking organization is pursuing. Innovations can create a competitive business advantage that is not limited to an economic advantage, it can delight customers and engage employees, create multidimensional business values as well. With well-educated digital workforce today, it's obvious that innovation is being pursued now more than ever, and in fact, we see much more innovations in more and more areas of the business landscapes. How to set guideline for running the business as a digital innovation powerhouse?

- **Innovation should benefit the widest possible audience within your organization:** Either change or innovation, people within the business ecosystem will have "What's In It For Me" mentality. Digital innovation is more often based on collective effort, and customer-centricity. From innovation management perspective, the latest digital technologies such as social computing make collaboration and sharing possible at large scale. Those who acquire the culture of sharing and collaborating will simply outperform those who don't. In essence, innovation is to figure out the better way to do things, and make it benefit broader participants. Besides those macro, large-scale problems, at the intermediate or micro level, for either organization or individual, how do you get motivated to be innovative at daily basis via solving real-world problems large or small, in a creative way? Innovation is not for its own sake, but for problem-solving. Looking uphill and into the future, can help to identify the real problems that matter, and on a scale that can make a significant difference for the longer term as well. Innovative organizations have deployed a range of different management, technology, process, and structural solutions:

-Earlier commercial involvement in project decision making, in an effort to enhance focus on commercially relevant compounds

-More rigorous procedures for portfolio management and more stringent criteria for the adoption of new projects

-Clearer guidelines for the handover from discovery to development, and for the integration of basic laboratory research with clinical trials and other applied research

-More sophisticated and comprehensive incentive and reward structures

-New structures that enable more external partnerships for discovery and the outsourcing of "non-core" activities.

- **Manage a balanced innovation portfolio to reap the business benefit for both short term and long run:** You aren't ignoring specific types of innovation. -Digital innovation has a broader spectrum with hybrid nature including incremental innovation, evolutionary innovation, and radical innovation; hard innovations such as products/service innovation, business model or process innovation, and soft innovations such as leadership innovation, communication innovation, and culture innovation. The gap between incremental and radical innovation is huge both in terms of outcomes if successful and on how to approach it. How to manage a balanced innovation portfolio depends on the nature and size of the business, as well as its capability-based innovation strategy. You aren't sacrificing the long-term viability of the innovation portfolio for only picking the low hanging fruits and gaining short-term rewards. Unfortunately, in most of the highly bureaucratic organizations, innovation is still serendipity. A mechanical enterprise that depends on doing something, again and again, engaging various teams and groups, have less appetite for change. Incremental innovation can be tolerated to some extent, but disruptive innovation is almost impossible until a change of the leadership is required to take initiatives for disruptive innovation. The true digital organizations are highly innovative, they master running a balanced innovation portfolio with the incremental improvement- radical innovation continuum.

- **Build a heterogeneous team to close three gaps in innovation management- idea gaps, collaboration gaps, and implementation gaps**: Build a heterogeneous team with a diversity of thoughts is the best way to close idea gaps; modern technology has made collaboration increasingly easy and seamless. The gap between collaboration and innovation is a big issue, especially in the booming world of collaboration software. Even after implementing a company-wide social collaboration platform, it probably never affects your innovation development directly. True collaboration doesn't happen as often as we'd like and people are sometimes afraid of letting go regarding of their title or whatever. It is also more difficult to just create human contact when the teams spread globally and/or if sharing values are still poor due to organization belonging importance. What also vexes most companies (and "innovators") is an implementation - commercialization of new ideas. That is why most innovation initiatives fail. People need to learn how to incubate and commercialize ideas more successfully. And in today's go-to-market business environment - the art of commercialization is becoming increasingly complex.

- **Create an innovation ecosystem with governance disciplines**: It is a common knowledge, that innovation management requires the highest risk-taking at a strategic value chain; including organization, investments, and assets. Create a disciplined, managed space for developing and testing new models, products, and business approaches, shielding innovation teams from the organization's dominant logic, established a standard, and operating procedures, which can stifle new thinking and approaches. It's also important to highlight the benefits of "interaction." Innovation is a non-linear process much akin to evolution. See innovation as a complex adaptive system, one can easily understand the value of placing ideas into an environment of interaction/collaboration where they can be tested and are having the opportunity to evolve.

- **Innovation needs the well-defined set of guidelines and rules for managing risks in a structural way:** Innovation is the development of a new combination of available resources, in a way that solves real-world problems in a more suitable way. The challenge is always about how to manage risk, build a healthy innovation portfolio, leverage resources, set priorities right and take steady pace to improve innovation success rate. You're accepting risk for potential reward. Digital brings both unprecedented opportunities and risks to the businesses today. Every innovation pursuit has a risk in it. Therefore, it is important to set guidelines for managing innovation and handling risk in a structural way. Although breaking outdated rules is an important part of innovation, 'business creativity' such as using creative thinking for business goals, does require certain 'rules.' To get the best results, you need to structure the creative process. Innovation is chaotic, messy, and uncertain only if you try to interpret innovation with conventional models. But when you will be able to define a new digital paradigm, the innovation doesn't seem so chaotic. It requires acknowledgment, involvement, and commitment. The principles and guidelines help to further frame processes, measures, and control.

Innovation must have an end result. It starts with managing business goals transparently together with innovation. If social collaboration, innovation management, and development processes are driven by clear strategic goals, the risks are easier to manage. This also enables co-creative processes not only to innovation but to business development overall. Achieving the above objectives requires a contracting process with clear stages, performance thresholds, and decision-making parameters combined with an iterative, experiential learning process that supports wide-ranging exploration at each stage.

2 Three Principles of Building a Creative Digital Workplace

Creativity is an inherent ability that cannot be taught, only developed.

Digital is the age of people, digital work environment needs to embrace the abundance of information and the culture of innovation, put people at the center of business, and both engage employees and delight customers. How can digital leaders set principles to encourage creativity, build creative digital workplaces and open the new chapter of digital innovations?

- **Encourage curiosity and shape digital mindsets:** Creativity is an innate ability to create novel ideas. Creativity in the workplace is fundamentally about the mental production of new ideas, not just any new ideas, but the creation of ideas that are both original and valuable. Everyone has the ability to create, but creativity is an inherent ability that cannot be taught, only developed. As businesses get more cut-throat in the hyper-connected working environment, this puts stress on the labor force that is not conducive to more creative and experimental thinking. But if you want to make a "creative culture," and build long-term business competency, you have to build a creative workplace which evokes the endless curiosity of its people and encourages the growth mindset for catalyzing changes. More specifically, a creative digital workplace will:

- Provide intellectual challenge and help people make progress.

-A place to strengthen their strength and expand their knowledge

-A change to apply their ideas and recognition for their ideas.

-A place people enjoy learning and doing, sharing insight and bringing wisdom.

- **Encourage people to question the status quo and think independently and create an environment that encourages dissent and candor:** Innovation is all about how to disrupt the old thinking and old way to do the things. Innovation is about seeing things from different angles or solving problems in different ways. It's about breaking down silos, and breaking through conventional wisdom. Innovation journey is like taking a hiking trip on the trail, only very few or even no people ever went before, and it takes courage and emotional maturity. Innovators are disruptive to the status quo, and often they are visionary as well, it means the seemly "misfit" nature of innovators is invaluable to push the business or the world getting out of the comfort zone, for advancement. Also, working with innovative individuals who have a strong sense of self has many benefits as well, because often they are authentic with independent thinking skills and clear thought processes, no hidden agenda, fewer rules, say what they mean and mean what they say, to keep things simple, because simplicity is one of the most important innovation principles.

- **Help people feel more comfortable with chaos, uncertainty, ambiguity, and develop creative capacity:** Due to the "VUCA" characteristics of digital new normal, digital workplace today needs to become dynamic and informative. The more innovative the employees are, the less tolerant of structure (policies, rules and paradigms) and less respectful of consensus one is. The workplace needs to be designed to help employees at all levels within an organization (from top leaders to front-line employees) understand and develop their creative capacity to solve problems and exploit opportunities in new and innovative ways. The emergent digital technologies and tools help to break of silo paradigms and loosen overly restricted structure, utilize cutting-edge narrow band psychometrics to diagnose, assess and train the core factors of creativity such as, cognitive processes, personality, motivation, capability, and build an open, hyperconnected and highly collaborative working environment for sowing innovation seeds, growing creativity fruits, and harvesting innovation abundance.

Digital workplace is fluid, live, creative and productive. Organizations need to invest in the cultivation of capacity for innovation. Mutual trust, innovative leadership, and emotional maturity are all critical in building a highly effective innovation workforce and workplace to achieve an exceptional result.

3 Three Core Principles of Accelerating Digital Innovation

Innovation comes from the Latin, "Innovare" - It means to change or alter things that already exist.

Innovation is the specific phenomenon of the knowledge-based economy. It is about having new knowledge and new processes. It is also about too much knowledge in terms of too many good creative ideas, and too little available resources. Innovation is about prioritization as well - via a systematic discipline that can "smell" the right idea at the right time and place, make it tangible, and achieve its business values.

- **Embrace cognitive differences**: People consciously or subconsciously protect their status quo. To be truly creative means challenging conventional wisdom and beliefs. It is likely that if you are creative, you will challenge the status quo as you push the parameters of the norms of life. To spark creativity and sow the seeds of innovation, inclusiveness is a necessity. Organizations with a command type of organizational culture are indifferent to external innovations and have innovation inertia. How to build a creative team and the associated issues are a matter of the corporate culture building and leadership effectiveness. The team's creativity is amplified via talented people with the cognitive difference that can understand things from different angles and bring new perspectives to the table. It is also about synchronizing of their individual inputs to make something that no one individual would achieve. It is more than that. It has its own dynamic that is in a state of constant flux. Hence, the exercise of blending people's problem-solving abilities to produce the desired outcome is a worthwhile thing to do. Further, most creative working environment and innovative organizations with real teamwork are headed by innovative and strong leaders with original ideas. The spirit comes from the top. The team's creativity is also inspired and motivated by such leaders, who can see, understand and appreciate the merits of different people and true inclusiveness.

- **Harness customer centricity**: Innovation is about transforming novel ideas and achieving its business value. Digital is the age of the customer. Customer-centric innovation is one of the focal points for digital organizations to thrive. The purpose of business is to create customers. Customer must be willing to pay for it, be it a product, process or service innovation. It must prove its value in the market. Listen to customers and involve them in the innovation process to gain insight and empathy. When managing innovation life cycle, customer involvement at all stages often elicits highly valuable information. Customers perhaps do not always know what they want for the next products or services, but they surely can provide insight into the goals, processes, and their contextual feedback is invaluable. Furthermore, have a deep understanding of the user through empathetic observation with the innovator using a more inductive approach as to what the customer wants to accomplish "next." Hence, customers are one of the most important links in the innovation process.

Harnessing customer-centricity is one of the core principles of digital innovation management.

- **Stay focus via prioritization setting**: Innovation is a disciplined approach to discovering and building opportunities in creating new meaningful sources of value to targeted users. With explosive information and continual digital disruptions, limited resources and fierce competitions, it's important to build business innovation strength and capabilities via prioritizing resources, managing risks with a portfolio management approach. Building a balanced innovation portfolio is a practical approach to optimizing resource and improving risk intelligence. Innovation is the sustainable and scalable way that can be learned and practiced. Leveraging tailored tools in effective innovation management is important to improve its success rate. Organizations with healthy innovation appetites, systematic innovation management approach with prioritization mechanism, and tailored innovation next practices will enjoy the balanced innovation portfolio with well-mixed radical innovation and incremental innovation projects, to maximize the business value and improve its innovation management success rate.

At the individual level, people have their own unique ways to spark creativity; at the organizational level, the business's innovation capability should be built via experimentation and taking systematic approaches. It's important to set up a team with cognitive differences, and its team members can proactively stimulate the new energy of fresh thinking. Even innovation management processes are systematic, innovation is also an "anti-status quo" flow, the processes shouldn't be too rigid to stifle innovation, but setting the right priority and laser focus on the most critical things which can make a difference to delight customers and innovate businesses at the dawn of the Digital Era.

4 Three "C's in Building an innovative team

Create and nurture an environment in your organization where curiosity is encouraged, and creative thinking is rewarded.

There are still full of serendipity in creativity: How many forms of creativity are there? How are they different? How are they similar? Isn't what makes them similar or different, also what makes them creativity? Creativity has many forms and manifestations. Take the standpoint that creativity has its starting point within an individual. Individual creativity is absolutely critical, but how to build a creative team to harness collective creativity?

- **Cognition:** Inclusiveness is a necessity to sow the seeds of innovation. The team members with the cognitive difference can understand things from a different angle, and bring the new perspective to the table. The exercise of blending people's problem-solving abilities to produce the desired outcome is a worthwhile thing to do. It is not just a mere accumulation of the creative inputs of those involved. It is also not only a synchronization of their individual inputs to make something that no one individual would achieve. It is more than that. It has its own dynamic that is in a state of constant flux. It builds up a momentum that draws creative contributions from the participants that they did not previously conceive or understood they were capable of.

- **Capacity**: Whether creativity can be collective is clear and flows from what seems like an expansive, generous, creative minds, how creative is the team depends on the creative capacity of its member. You can get a diverse group of people together in one room and still not have "creativity" if the participating individuals are not particularly creative. What matters is how creative are the individuals. The tool utilizes cutting-edge narrow band psychometrics to diagnose, assess and train the core factors of creativity namely: Cognitive processes, personality, motivation, and capacity. The workplace needs to be designed to help employees at all levels within an organization (from leaders to front-line) understand and develop their creative capacity to solve problems and exploit opportunities in new and innovative ways.

- **Culture**: Once we take into consideration the influences around the workforce (environment, culture, principles, etc.), how to build a creative team and the associated issues are a matter of the corporate culture building and leadership effectiveness. Most of the creative teams and innovative organizations with real teamwork are headed by strong leaders with original ideas. The spirit comes from the top. The team's creativity is inspired and motivated by the leaders, who see, understand and appreciate the merits of different people. If there are no inspiring ideas, people's motivation is reduced. In creative organizations with highly innovative leadership, people are encouraged and given the time resources to work on new things that excite them, all are required to produce new ideas, people are often trained in creative methods and techniques, the business model is often challenged, everyone has a personal creativity objective at work and there is much humor to go around, fewer office politics, more professional learning, and sharing.

Given the nature of most companies, the integration of the art and science of creativity is proportional to the need to maintain and increase the bottom line. All humans are naturally creative. Create and nurture an environment in your organization where curiosity is encouraged, and creative thinking is rewarded. The great leaders understand this and with that understanding, they build an innovative culture and take their organizations to the pinnacle of unbelievable success of innovation.

5 The Principles and Practices to Encourage Creativity

The solution to encourage creativity is to maximize use of employees' brainpower.

As businesses get more cut-throat in the face of fierce competitions and unprecedented changes, this puts stress on the labor force that is not conducive to creative, experimental thinking. As a business leader, what are the common solutions to encourage creativity? Will you allow people to make mistakes? Spend time on something with no guarantee of ROIs? Work on what interests them? Which type of work activities, roles, industries, requires great deals of creativity? How do you, as leaders involve all people in creative thinking and actions? And how can you help improve the harvest of the creative seeds? Doesn't the real solution to innovation or creativity begin with inquiry? Would it not be prudent to focus on ensuring all levels of the organization are well founded on asking learning questions?

- **The solution to encourage creativity is to maximize use of employees' brainpower:** This mindset will build on the wisdom. It's the "WOW" moment where the light bulb in your brain turns on to realize your brilliance as an individual or as a leader. Creativity has a language, but it is altogether different from the one found in the business environment. Generally speaking, you must allow room for failure, for tangents, for "being different." Every person has an unknown amount of creativity, innovation, and productivity as well as an unknown amount of intelligence, knowledge, experience, and energy. All of these come from the brain. How much of this brainpower employees will unleash on their work depends almost totally on the leadership and corporate culture. But most businesses value monoculture. Creativity is a long-term endeavor. It must be cultivated, but most businesses measure success at the end of every growth cycle. The leadership exercises a key role in the careful planning of activities to build the interdisciplinary nature of the team, to promote collective creativity while maintaining the high tension of the group to the new, the easy-going projects, the belief that operates according to the trajectory of human progress and to be able to contribute to their professional effort.

- **The best way to foster creativity is to help people communicate in a way that instills confidence, not fear**: Creativity is an individual activity. It is, by nature, unique to each person. There is no template that you can apply and suddenly has a creative workforce. It must be done slowly, patiently, and individually. That is why so many companies won't do it. Allow autonomy; let people choose how and on what they work. At the organizational level, collective creativity needs to be orchestrated via building a culture with following characteristics:

  - Create a safe environment for learning from failure
  - Provide intellectual challenge to stimulate thinking and help people make progress
  -Foster integrity, trust, and transparency
  - Encourage curiosity and a growth mindset
  -Make people feel more comfortable with chaos, uncertainty, and ambiguity
  -Encourage people to question the status quo
  -Create an environment that encourages dissent and candor
  - Allow time for play and experimentation
  - Establish clear, shared goals

- **Develop a 'Center of Excellence for Creativity' to harness innovation:** It is a virtual team, consisting of a specified number of the diversity of thought and experience. Managers are nominated by this team from various functions for a specific period, and they work on this team in addition to their regular responsibilities. This team has a leader who is also in a rotating position. This team works with various ideas and makes a regular presentation to the management of successes achieved; it provokes, supports, provides direction when needed and give others time, space and freedom to create. A "CoE" of innovation helps to create:
  - A "place" to expand their knowledge
  - A chance to apply their ideas
  - A recognition of the ideas
  - No embedding behavior in the office
  - Build a collaboration culture in the company

- **Encourage diversity of thought and non-egalitarian review:** The best way to end up where everybody else is, is to follow the majority guidance on where to go at every turn. Another way to say this is: If someone is telling you that they have a map to your destination, then you can be certain that you will not arrive at any place new. Organizations need to allow time for a number of different 'creative' activities or opportunities to suit different types of people. In the same way, that people have different 'learning' styles, they also have different innovation styles. Creativity is a synthesis of two qualities: Imagination with which you create new ideas and the concreteness with which you can transform ideas into real works. Some of us are mostly imaginative, other practical: very small number of people possesses both qualities in equal. It is possible to build creative groups in which, under the guidance of a charismatic leader, visionary people work together synergistically with practical people to achieve collective creativity.

- **Applying the principle such as "Innovation as a Top Priority" to develop talent management practices**: If an organization believes ' Innovation as a process of value creation,' and ensures that people are aligned to this belief, the chances of success increases substantially. First, people who are being considered for elevation or promotion must have a minimum score for 'Creativity' through a well-designed assessment and evaluation process. Second, every individual who is promoted to a pre-designated level must compulsorily go through a training program on 'Creativity and Innovation,' before taking up the responsibility of the new position. Lastly, as a part of the onboarding process, every new employee must go through a training program on 'Innovation.' In a highly innovative environment, leaders can focus on vision/mission/top-goals/budgets and on leading (for real) – and will stand out stronger. Managers can focus on managing only what is important and relevant to the results, and will be able to focus and deliver maximum results/information (both up/down and down/up) without being stressed out. People can use their full potential in a stress-free and truly co-operative environment.

There is no one global or universal solution to building innovation and creativity at the organizational level. It's business leaders' responsibility to establish an environment with a high-risk tolerance, where people can grow and develop, be curious and creative without fear. It's the management that can strike the right balance between increasing productivity and encouraging innovation; between setting standard and letting "out-of-the-box" thinking flow; between risk management and risk tolerance; between discovering the new way to do things and "we always do things like that" attitude; and it's about optimizing control and improving working pleasure. It is a journey to climb the mountain also enjoys the scenes.

6 Five Principles of Business Innovation

Being innovative is more important than any specific innovation. Innovativeness is a way of thinking.

We're approaching the world with complexity, hyperconnectivity, and the highest level of education ever, and as a result, more people are competing in an increasingly competitive global arena. With the exponential growth of information and well-educated digital workforce today, it's obvious that innovation is being pursued now more than ever, and in fact, we see much more innovation in more and more areas of the business landscapes as a result of an increasingly well-educated population across the globe.

- **Being innovative is more important than any specific innovation**: Innovativeness is a way of thinking. While the change was often previously discrete, intermittent, and predictable, it is now constant, discontinuous, and unpredictable, so we need to change the way we change. This is where absorptive capacity, dynamic capabilities, learning agility, etc, are needed. We don't really know the future of the industry or the environment, but we prepare ourselves to create it better and compete in it. Innovation is the idea brought to market even when other people thought the idea was crazy or too obvious, and later when it leads to success, everyone looks at and says, "I wish I had thought of that!"

- **Looking at innovation from the perspective of developing business-wide innovation capabilities:** This requires an effective 'innovation system' that is capable of supporting both widespread incremental innovation in products/services and ways of working as well as the rarer 'step-change' innovation in products/services, working methodology, business model, and market positioning. Innovation has three phases: Discovery of a problem or new idea, designing a prototype solution and the ultimate delivery of a commercially astute outcome. That the best point of view is to see innovation as a system, capable of delivering organization-wide capability. If you look at all the attempts over the last few decades to create a mutually exclusive and collectively exhaustive typology for innovation, you will soon realize that it is probably not possible given that almost every area of human endeavor is subject to change and thus "innovation."

- **Businesses need to determine where best to focus their innovation activities**: From a business perspective, 'anything new to your business' is an effective definition to encourage both large and small ideas and ideas that are new and 'copied with pride' from others. If it brings increased value to the business, then that's what's important, not semantics. Establishing sustained and institutional-level innovation is the goal. Innovation consists of two phases: The creative, ideation up front, and then the sharing and implementation downstream when explaining, developing, and selling to sufficiently involve others in adopting and improving upon the "excitement" are involved. In other words, the "moment of Eureka" may be very exciting, but hanging on for the long-term adoption and extended use phases may become quickly challenging and exhausting. So, it pays to learn to view innovation matters realistically.

- **Successful innovation is finding a bridge between 'push' and 'pull'**: Commercial implementation may be represented by creating a need for or finding a need for a 'pull.' To build that bridge requires enthusiasm, belief, determination and commitment as well as a good business case. Innovation is not so much a system, although you need to have processes in place, but more a responsive way of working in general. The minimum requirement for innovation is that the product, process, marketing method or organizational method must be new (or significantly improved) to the firm. This includes products, processes, and methods that firms are the first to develop and those that have been adopted by other firms or organizations. "Pushing" only is not efficient to drive innovation, because idea creation scenario takes brainstorming, collaboration, knowledge absorbing and insight capture.

- **'Innovation Agility' enables people to see and solve problems in flexible and adaptive ways:** It is about incorporating entrepreneurial and startup principles, with a focus on reducing risk adversity to add value to the quality of people's lives. This involves thinking systemically because it involves organizational climate, culture, and process changes, simultaneously, within a business ecosystem context. Innovation as the creation and development of new ideas cause meaningful change for customers and the company. This isn't always a new product or service but can also be an improvement in processes, employee satisfaction or the environmental impact. If it makes your employees happier and customers more satisfied, the firm will eventually also benefit from that!

Innovation is the development of a new combination of available resources, in a way that solves problems of others in a more suitable way. Using the principles of adaptive innovation, shaping innovative mindsets, building innovation capability, and cultivating innovation agility are all crucial to making innovation management more practical than just serendipity.

7 Three guidelines to Build a Workplace with Creative Tension

You can feel creative tension when you sense the freedom to be creative, the harmony not via compliance only, but through brainstorming.

Digital is the age of innovation. Creativity is, by nature, unique to each person. There is no template which you can apply and suddenly have a creative workforce or manage innovation without hassles. That is why so many companies won't do it. However, in competing for the long run and focus on the top line business growth, building a creative workforce and mastering innovation management should be put on the business agenda of every top business executive and talent manager. In practice, what's the "express" of an innovative culture? And how to set the digital principles in building a creative workplace with creative tension? Creative tension - when you see it, do you know it?

- **Stepping out of comfort zone effortlessly:** As we all know the only "Certainty" or a "Constant" is "CHANGE." Business is only an extended part of our life and all businesses have to accept change to survive. Uncertainty per se is not a problem; it poses a risk for those who have a fixed mindset and creates opportunities for those with a growth mindset. The fact is that people's belief system on a subconscious level is slowly "adjust" to a new set of principles rather than the conscious level. In any case, behavioral change in organizations happens on a group level and a person's "resistance" is just the symptom of an "organizational allergy" to the loss of the previously set operational equilibrium. Innovation becomes possible only if people can step out of their comfort zone. In fact, innovative solutions often come from the floor and not the ceiling. Therefore, organizations need to support the process of improvisation, and organizational leaders should have the "sense and sensitivity" to read the culture expression - have you seen the creative tension due to abundance of information flow and the diversity of thoughts, and can you build a culture to encourage idea sharing and risk-taking, but discourage unprofessional competitions?

- **Ask open questions to explore new possibilities frequently:** To spark creativity, your digital workforces with heterogeneous team setting include all sorts of thinkers: Creative thinker, critical thinker, systems thinker, holistic thinker, etc. They would complement each other's thought processes and amplify the collective human capabilities. They make creative communication often via asking open questions to explore new possibilities. Creative Thinkers live out of the box or bigger box; ask open questions such as "Why Not," or "What If," to collect relevant information. Critical Thinkers are always chasing root cause via asking the big 'WHY' questions without too rushing up into "HOW." Understand through asking the right questions, and open to varying answers. They not only ask the right questions, but rather absorb information forecast potentials; risks/benefits; mitigation and compare and contrast options, facts, ideas against logic and creativity.

- **Deal with innovation dilemmas strategically:** Modern businesses operate in such a complex and uncertain digital dynamic ecosystem, the business leaders and professionals have to understand the creative tension, handle management paradox and deal with innovation dilemmas strategically. Often, they have to take a balanced approach to maintaining coherence, while allowing autonomy; strike a balance between exploration and exploitation; compensate short-term and short-range attention of daily operations, with a long-term broad-range vision, that could steer the organization in the right direction through uncharted water and blurred digital territories. A mindful or thoughtful leader has a better perception to deal with complex issues and manage innovation via tailored approach, upon thinking profoundly, and upon striking the right balance without any sort of extreme thinking or bias. Innovation is about thinking differently, acting differently, delivering differently, and adding value differently from the status quo. Innovation requires thinking beyond, as opposed to outside the box, altering or changing the frame of reference to create previously unconsidered solutions.

It is important to build a culture of innovation and encourage free thinking and experimenting. Part of creating an organizational environment that facilitates creativity involves paying attention to employee wellbeing and building individual emotional intelligence to generate more positive emotions and reducing unnecessary organizational pressures, have the right dose of creative tension and healthy competition to spark innovation. Metaphorically, the company is like a ship, the sea is the volatile environment, the old world is the industrial age and the new world is the digital era. You don't have any choices but to change your sails to move forward. You cannot go back to the old world as it is the ship going to the new world. And the only way to get there is by using change techniques and leveraging innovation mechanism. If you stagnate you don't grow and your company doesn't grow. It is the responsibility of each leader to examine themselves and to make sure they are open to true understanding and explore the new digital innovation adventure.

8 The "PEARL" Creativity Principles

Always dig through the thoughts underneath the words, and be authentic of being who you are!

Creativity is the high level of thinking and innovation is the light businesses are pursuing. We all just fumble around from the dark to chase new ideas. Is there such a magic formula to double or triple of your innovative ability? Should you follow the "PEARL" principles for living with creativity?

Profundity   Excellence   Authenticity   Resilience   Logic

Figure 5 The "PEARL" Creativity Principle

- **Profundity:** Back to the root of the word "profundity," it means to be insightful and understanding. The digital ecosystem is dynamic with velocity, it's important to fill cognitive gaps and spark the fountain of collective creativity via profound thoughts and inclusive culture. However, often at the traditional business setting with an overly restrictive hierarchy, people normally 'close' the boundaries of the system, so that less energy is transferred and, therefore, fewer changes happen in the system, little creativity gets inspired, and the little box called comfort zone turns to become one of the biggest roadblocks to innovation. To keep the digital flow, leadership profundity and wisdom have to be enforced by practicing multidimensional thinking such a critical thinking and embracing holism and nonlinearity. Innovation effectiveness is dependent on how capable the business can manage changes and keep the digital flow. Because workers now are more educated than what they used to be, they are at least more informed as to what is going on and the changes taking place around them. It is the responsibility of each leader to examine themselves and to make sure they are open to true understanding. Climbing Knowledge-Insight-Wisdom pyramid is an important step in gaining profundity and reaching the next level of innovation management maturity.

- **Excellence**: A progressive mind is to make continuous improvement either through creativity or excellence. Achieving excellence is more about "perfecting," not about "perfection." There's a word of difference between the noun 'perfect' with the implication of a 'perfect' entity and the verb 'perfecting,' through progressive problem-solving.

The key is striking a balance between opposing forces, each with its own set of pros and cons. Excellence mind can cultivate innovation, but perfectionism may diminish enthusiasm and slows down progress, or leads to analysis paralysis and no endpoint at all. Striving for perfection is an asset to the implementation of an idea while at the same time it is a detriment to the idea's creation. For the works need a certain level of creativity, and whose creations and output do not require precision, you should spend more time on brainstorming, no need for wasting precious time striving for perfection. Instead, good enough, will be and is good enough when bringing innovative, inventive products and services to the marketplace!

- **Authenticity:** Being authentic means to discover "Who You Are," your inner strength and personal traits. Being original is one of the important characteristics of authenticity because you don't just blindly follow other people's opinions or conventional wisdom. You discover and explore your own path. Originality means creative and independent thinking. In other words, make your own mind up, or formulate your own conclusions, ideas, or expressions. Originality is valuable as authenticity. Original thinking is independent, creative, original, special or different. This world needs more original thinkers than ever to handle the ever-increasing complexities, and organizations need to be able to recognize them not least in order to innovate and adapt. The traits like, character, self-motivation, creativity, uniqueness and confidence can be the indicator of original thinking which is also a trait of being authentic. The organization and our society will become more naturally digital fit with an abundance of authenticity. When digital professionals are inspired to discover who they are, their inner genius, and empowered to grow into who they want to be, the negative emotions and unhealthy competitions are discouraged and every member can bring some wisdom to the workplace.

- **Resilience**: There is no innovation without failure. And there is no great leadership without resilience. Digital leaders and professionals must have resilient mindsets in order to adapt to continuous digital disruptions or unexpected setbacks either in career or personal life. Resilience is the ability to respond to change, dare to be creative when facing difficulties, recover quickly from setbacks, and the capacity to respond to the unexpected in a way that increases gain or minimizes loss. Resilience is about B.O.U.N.C.E. It's about regaining one's footing which could be bouncing back, forwards or restructuring your life integrating the change in some way that works. It's also about being able to keep working and focusing, even during stress and disturbances, rather than reacting to stressful situations. A person with resilience lives in a grounded and centered place, being flexible and adaptable in the midst of adversity, threat, and stress. It's an important trait to be an innovator and a digital leader today.

- **Logic**: Creativity and logic seem to be opposite. In fact, it's not unless you misunderstand the logic with conventional wisdom. Logic is not always linear or just blindly following the authority's opinion. Logic is part of the deep universal structure of all languages and meaningful human behaviors. Creativity is not the opposite of logic, in fact, logic is a deep part of creativity through connecting unusual dots. Innovativeness is not just about styles or fashions, it is the state of mind embedded with nonlinear logic. And logic can be abstracted across disciplinary domains as well. Logic was discovered, much as we discover mathematical truths. Fundamentally, thoughts, words, and actions, in this order - this is the logical way to be either creative or persuasive. People, even well trained digital professionals or leaders today often confuse the means with the end or substance with style, they need to retool the mind and think in a more logical way.

Creativity is a flow, an abstract and an imagination. You can put creativity in a box and say, it's "all just creativity," or you can pull it out of the box and look at it through different lenses. It's your perception. Set your own principle, practice, practice, and practice more to spur the abundance of creativity.

Chapter 3

Digital Innovators

Innovators find more viewing spots than the rest.

With the increasing speed of changes, fierce competition, and unprecedented uncertainty and ambiguity, creativity is the most wanted skill in the Digital Era. But who are the innovators? Do innovators belong to a rare breed, or are innovators just among us and within us? With "VUCA" characteristics, what are important personas do digital innovators present?

- **The bigger-box thinker:** Creativity is analogized as "Out-of-the-Box" thinking, more precisely, innovators today need to be bigger-box-thinkers, because the borders of functions, firms, industries and geographical regions are blurring due to the latest digital technologies. Being a digital innovator means you need to break down silo thinking, break through conventional wisdom and challenge the status quo, push and encourage yourselves and the entire team to "think in bigger boxes" (think outside of your job description and consider company, industry, and even societal impacts). Being a bigger box thinker also means to leverage nonlinear thinking and let the creative mind run free for a while, engage all people in the team for improving both thought processes and optimizing working processes. Assume that every problem has multiple solutions and ask yourself and others for both framing the right questions and managing alternative and better ways to solve them. Thinking in bigger-box also means you need to be in a continuous learning mode with interdisciplinary understanding, embrace critical thinking and creative thinking to challenging existing thoughts or standards and to seek additional knowledge and experience,

- **The pathfinder:** Being creative also means you need to get used to stepping outside that old box to unfamiliar territory, you discover and explore your own path. An innovator is often a visionary and a pathfinder. Because innovation comes with a foresight to envision a need that others overlook or ignore and a willingness to forge ahead to satisfy visions, in spite of a risk of failure. Pathfinders are on the continuous journey of discovery. The word "Discovery" refers to "Knowledge," or more precisely, insight, you discover something others ignore, or you take the path without just following in others' footsteps. Discovery is 'the journey of life' as each day; we discover something previously unknown to us. Discovery is the choice to look at something differently and by that choice never look at anything the same. Vision grows for those who learn to see and enter into the experience of simple perceptual connection with the wide open personal completion into the moment's happening. As one develops full participation at the moment, so does the perceptual envisioning dexterity, expanding reception and reach. The world needs more of creative thinkers who can handle the ever-increasing complexities and discover the new path for leading digital transformation.

- **The multidimensional viewer:** Innovators find more viewing spots than the rest. They find angles to wiggle through where most are unable to even envision a place where there is an angle. They have the ability to connect the unusual dots and see things through the broader lens. In short, innovators obviously think differently, and problem-solving is part of their DNA. Creative minds with cognitive differences are good at asking open and thought-provoking questions because the good question brings multifaceted perspective. Creative people are typically disrespectful of outdated rules, and their creativity is really their way of breaking out of or reframing how they see the world and try to push the world forward.

Creativity is a high level of thinking and intelligence. Intelligence is the quick and clear perception of any situation, plus ability to adjust to any circumstances. It is contextual and multidimensional. Digital innovators also present leadership skills, master creative communication, understand what is wrong with the status quo, have the good sense and sound judgment to attract and surround themselves with the right people, and work collaboratively to do more with innovation.

An innovator has an obligation to...

An innovator has an obligation to her/his vision, to be authentic and to think strategically.

- An innovator has an obligation to his/her vision, to be forward thinking; and convince others to take the risks that true innovation requires.

- An innovator has an obligation to challenge the status quo, for social, humanity and commercial betterment.

- An innovator has an obligation to "be a natural creative thinker." True innovations come out from within; they are not only original but self-satisfying to the initiator.

- An innovator has an obligation to think strategically since such innovation initiatives are generated out of some real concerns, purposes and objectives to implement the application for more durability.

- An Innovator has an obligation to be open, to share and question, to challenge existing concepts, and to bring the new perspective, fresh idea or insight.

- An innovator has the obligation to evoke emotion in the products/services/knowledge he or she produces, because they embody the enthusiasm of the innovator, with the purpose to build a strong brand.

- An innovator has an obligation to be authentic; never take decisions against his/her own ideological and aesthetic principles.

An innovator has an obligation to love the nature; with the responsibility to ensure that the solution is eco-friendly and sustainable. An innovator has an obligation to focus on one singular outcome: Does the innovation positively benefit the earth and its inhabitants now and in the long-term? If this is the viability of the product, you're not only onto a winner but also part of the change that's needed.

1 Five Traits of Innovators

You cannot make omelets without breaking some eggs.

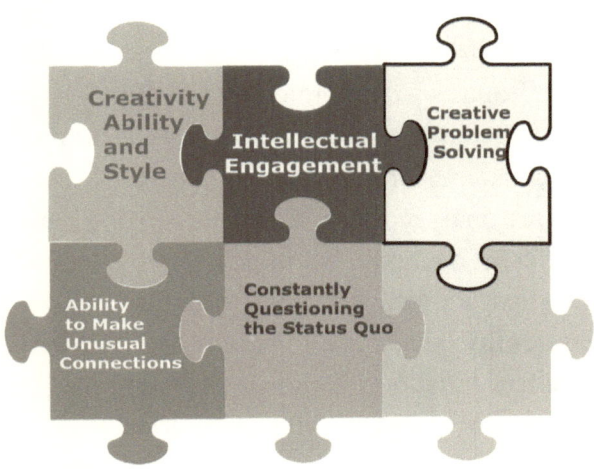

Figure 6 Five Traits of Innovators

Creativity is the #1 wanted quality for digital leaders and professionals nowadays, but where can you discover innovators? Do innovators belong to rare breed or are they among us and within us? Why can innovators find more view spots than others? Why can innovators think differently via connecting unusual dots? What are important traits of innovators?

- **Cognitive ability and style:** Cognition is a faculty for processing of information, applying knowledge, and changing preferences. Cognition can happen in many different ways and their combinations. Enhancing our "description of the world and ourselves within it," is cognition and it differs from ordinary (usually habitual) thoughts. The cognition involves exploring varieties of meanings/thoughts, abandoning old connections, and establishing new relations. In neuronal terms, this involves disabling some of the "wiring" and working on the new ones. All of that requires a deliberate mental effort. Cognition, or cognitive processes, can be natural or artificial, conscious or unconscious. These processes are analyzed from different perspectives within different contexts. All of us have a creative/artistic side while also have a curious/scientific side. As all humans are bestowed with three basic instincts which are humility (egoless awareness and acceptance), curiosity (restlessness with the status quo), and creativity (urge to change/improve the status quo). Amazingly, these three basic instincts are intertwined. Humility energizes curiosity and curiosity ignites creativity. In simple words, without humility, curiosity is feeble and without curiosity, creativity is ineffectual.

- **Intellectual engagement**: Creativity relates to intelligence, empathy, idealism, process understanding, communication skills, cultural understanding, leadership, and definitely - understanding what is wrong with the status quo. Spotting and scoring individual as an innovator needs to focus on individual capabilities and potential to innovate. Select the indicators to assess the intrinsic capacity of individuals such as, interdisciplinary skills and knowledge, plasticity (fast learning), and synthesizing capability. When we explore the mental process of acquiring new knowledge through thoughts, experiences, and senses - The actual "thinking" is a conscious or non-conscious effort to reorganize your memories (meanings) and integrate newly acquired knowledge (new meanings). The conscious effort employs and tries to expand one's attention span to stay focused on the wide range of meanings (memories) in order to reconcile them into a coherent whole. Innovative leaders assimilate all relevant and available information, transform them into business insight, consciously cultivate a culture of innovation, and make effective decisions for the organization they lead.

- **Creative problem-solving**: Creative minds with cognitive differences can reframe questions before answering them, to focus on WHY, before getting to the HOW. The good question is usually open and thought-provoking: The good question brings multifaceted perspective. Creative people are typically disrespectful of outdated rules, and their creativity is really their way of breaking out of or reframing how they see the world. In short, innovators obviously think differently- problem-solving is part of their DNA whether it is in the invention, marketing, repurposing something already being there. Creative leaders also have the ability to reframe the circumstances or conditions around a problem, to solve a problem creatively. As far as leading change is concerned, there is a lot of crossover between change leadership and creativity (tolerance for ambiguity/idea generation/confidence etc.). The leadership team with a cognitive difference will have better capability and complementary skills to solve problems creatively and lead business transformation effortlessly.

- **Ability to make unusual connections**: Creativity is all about connecting the dots. It's an inner process to create novel ideas. Creativity may start with the biological basis of creativity (nature); then the development or suppression of those characteristics during maturation (nurture); then the biological and social support of those traits (nutrition). Innovators find more viewing spots than the rest. Creative leaders will build up the working environment to nurture creativity, enable dot-connecting activities such as cross-functional collaboration, and encourage the freedom of thinking and action.

- **The tendency to constantly question the status quo:** Innovation is about thinking differently, acting differently, delivering differently, and adding value differently from the status quo. Innovation requires thinking beyond, as opposed to outside the box, altering or changing the frame of reference to create previously unconsidered solutions. Innovators need to rise above the status quo and take on a new set of activities that have them involved in the strategy development process from the get-go. Hence, innovators are also better business strategists.

Innovators are at their very heart visionaries who also have determination, dedication, passion, curiosity, inspiration and motivation. Innovation comes with a foresight to envision a need that others overlook or ignore and a willingness to forge ahead to satisfy visions, in spite of a risk of failure. They are authentic and confident. If you're not sure of yourself, you won't be able to convince others to follow your leadership and vision. Innovators are the rare breed, but innovators are also among us and within us.

2 Top Qualities and Skills of Innovation Leaders

Innovative leaders today are digital conductors, problem-solvers, and culture influencers.

There are many common leadership qualities or skills shared between an innovative leader and any good leader or any creative team member. However, being an innovative leader takes more courage, creativity, strength, collaboration, and concentration.

- **An innovative leader must walk the tightrope between diplomat and maverick:** On one hand, innovative leaders will get faster results by respecting people, getting the best effort from the people; listening and orchestrating as fast as possible. On the other hand, to deliver innovation projects on time, they must be willing to take risks, and jump through some hoops. Knowing that success will reward and failure will punish. You cannot make omelets without breaking some eggs. Walking that tightrope makes the innovation leader a likable acrobat; a true artist; in short, an innovation leader.

- **An innovative leader must be like a conductor leading the innovative orchestra with a not yet completely written symphony:** Creativity, openness for the new ideas, out of the box thinking and very strong capacity for a rapid integration and digestion of abundant information all come from various sources (technology, service, business, financials, etc.). Also, an innovative leader has the skill to extract and impart learning from any situation, successes as well as failures, humor, mainly self-humor.

- **An innovative leader is technology-savvy and digital fluent**: It's also important that innovation leaders and innovators understand both the technology they are using to serve customers and the strategy of the business. It's key to combining technical knowledge with business understanding. Innovative development team members exhibit qualities that make them better able to generate or discover good ideas, have the fair judgment to know what's important, and have the leadership ability to deliver.

- **An innovative leader today is a problem-solver, who has to create, manage, and exploit innovation networks and business eco-system:** Leaders who can recognize innovative ideas, fight for resources and political cover, and connect ideas and teams together to deliver an innovative result are also critical to achieving innovation excellence. In order to select the right people to drive innovation projects, you must recognize that in today's environment you're no longer sourcing all the innovation inside your company. Innovation is a process that is cross-functional and non-industry specific. It is, at its heart, a problem-solving process - and as such you need to find someone who is able to network the firm to uncover the problems, to get problem owners on board with the innovation program, and then, to devise the appropriate mix of processes, people, and tools to solve the problem and execute the solution.

- **An innovative leader has the transdisciplinary knowledge and cross-functional experience**: Innovative leaders emerge from many functional backgrounds, to network into non-conventional connections, out of the team's discipline and usual networks; with the ability to irradiate inclusion. Successful innovation team leaders offer the ability to:
  - Clarify the opportunity and articulate the vision
  - Develop and manage the process of innovation
  - Promote a healthy climate for innovation
  - Inspire team members to create a portfolio of new ideas, concepts and scenarios (through 'exploratory thinking' methods)
  - Coach team members on innovation management practices and how to overcome the barriers to innovation

- **Innovative leaders' skills are varying**: The first question is what type of innovation your company's seeking. You need different types of people for various innovation objectives (incremental, breakthrough, etc.) for different types of companies (solutions versus products, etc.). Aptitude and skills will vary from front-end to back-end. Typically no one has them all and the first sign of a good innovation leader is he/she will recognize his/her limitations and build a team to compensate. The desired skills may include:

Innovative Leadership Skills	Description
(1) A real capability to listen and integrate each function's inputs	The projects get enriched and solid while progressing in its development.
(2) A deep understanding of key consumer/ customer insights	An excellent memory and courage not to forget those key findings when moving ahead in the execution.
(3) Communication to promote ideas	Innovative leaders need a large and deep structure of soft skills, such as the ability to communication, conflicts resolution, empowerment, motivational skills, control of criticism, etc.
(4) Project and Program Management skills	Innovative leaders champion how new initiatives get framed and then expertly guide engineers/managers/ marketers through the cross-functional development and commercialization stage gates to produce real results in a timely manner that lead to the creation of new business value.
(5) Facilitation	Innovative leaders explore,

skills	promote and even translate new conversations to stakeholders at all levels that lead to new service/product programs
(6) A high-level social intelligence	Add the elements of collaboration and social network experience. If you're doing this as a collaborative process, you need to be able to build, maintain, and engage internal and external social networks to provide new sources of insights, experiences, and ideas that drive value for the company.

Table 1 Innovative leadership skills

Therefore, the effective innovation leaders should well mix the soft leadership qualities and hard business/technology expertise, with strong focus, perseverance, and capabilities of doing the opposite of the crowd with confidence!

3 T-Shaped Talent with Innovative Thinking

Innovative thinkers are explorers and synthesizers of new world-views, or future views of the world.

With the border between different functions or disciplines continues blurring, the specialized generalists are in strong demand, or we normally call the "T-Shape" talent, and the innovative thinker. You start with a strong T and then sprinkle heavy dots randomly across the graph with varying strengths of lines connecting them and the occasional pulsing outlier dots. How do T-shaped people feel? What are their emotional strengths and weaknesses? What is their ability to make sense of a situation? Does this "profile-metaphor" take into account fit and affinity, rapport and empathy? Why are T-shaped professionals so popular and how to groom such type of talent?

- **Many talent people start to build T-shaped skills when they progress through their career:** People start out broad and narrow. As they progress through their career, they start to become T-shaped, either because they've gotten experienced in a specific area based upon where they work and the opportunities presented, or because they've established themselves as very strong reputation, in particular, topic area. As they progress even further, they could become square or rectangular shaped and become more deeply skilled in many different areas, if they stayed in an area of practices that allowed them to do so. When they started to climb to certain areas of management, etc, those hands-on skills may not get to be put to the task as much, and some of their skills may atrophy, not be current, but they're gaining strength and expertise in new areas as they continue to grow, and build the recombinant capability, like onion - one layer over the other, etc.

- **The people who helped to shape our world are some of the broadest and innovative thinkers:** The progress of the world is pushed forward by a select few who were applying agile techniques, using broad and diverse skills to create the impossible. For some reason having a broad and wide set of skills are now frowned upon. Yet it is these broad skills that helped to shape the world. As we go through the digital and information revolution, we must embrace the skills of the past to build the new capabilities, and refocus on the problems we are solving and use any number of skills and disciplines to get there. To create the new requires not just one skill, but many, not just old experience, but the new perspective. However, you must operate like a T-shaped individual, have one skill which is your anchor, and look wide from there. Plus, like Thomas Edison realized, you cannot do it on your own, no matter how broad your skills, you still need a diverse team of talented people who help bring all sorts of strengths and capabilities together.

- **Innovative thinking is a mindset that needs to transcend departmental, even industry verticals:** There are collaborative benefits of the co-design approach, so the breadth and depth of the 'T' in the context of a team has to respond to a challenge. That means a blend of skills and experience can be fostered in different ways. In addition, we need the broad exposure and some deep expertise that come with the "T," but we also need strong interpersonal communication and collaboration skills in order to build an innovative team, with qualities such as, resilience, empathy, metacognition, critical thinking, relationship building, agility, and community participation.

- **Innovative thinkers are explorers and synthesizers of new world-views, or future views of the world:** The "T" metaphor was not made to tell us how much we know about something or how many areas we know about. It was made instead to illustrate a predisposition to diversify our focus or not. Usually, we are either "experts" or "explorers," and in the fast-changing digital era, perhaps you need to become both. We've got stuck in the "T" metaphor and we are now trying to say that what distinguishes people is the types of expertise they own. The "T" metaphor is something invented to talk the talk of managers in over specialized industrial settings giving the notion that one could start using a design way of thinking, leaving the old industrial system untouched. However, the focus should be on the capability of innovative thinkers to contribute to particular professional practices in specific contexts, rather than to focus on individual behaviors or decontextualized skills or knowledge.

- **The "T model" is more about resource management, not just about expertise or knowledge management:** Knowledge is N-dimensional, skill is multidimensional, and responsibility is comparatively most likely to be one-dimensional. It makes more sense to think of responsibility being specialized than it does to think of "expertise" being specialized. "Mastery" is being the default state of an expert specialist, but even mastery makes sense mainly in a pragmatic and contextualized way, not in an essentially inherent way. One has to be able to build connections between the areas of specialization, to cross over so to speak. This is like becoming a skilled translator. It is not enough to know each language well; one has to build a network of connections and contrasts between the two languages, so that as one translates, one can experience flow.

Due to the hyper-connected and transcendental nature of the digital age, either you are expert or explorer, continuously expanding knowledge horizon becomes more strategic and tactical for mastering professional skills and building transferable capabilities. Go broader before dive in, or dig deeper, and then gain interdisciplinary insight to understand things from different angle or perspective, that's the growth mind adapting to the change and getting more popular in the digital era.

4 Nine Aspects of Creative Leadership

Creative leadership can be described as "Adaptability meets Agility" and "Innovation meets Principles."

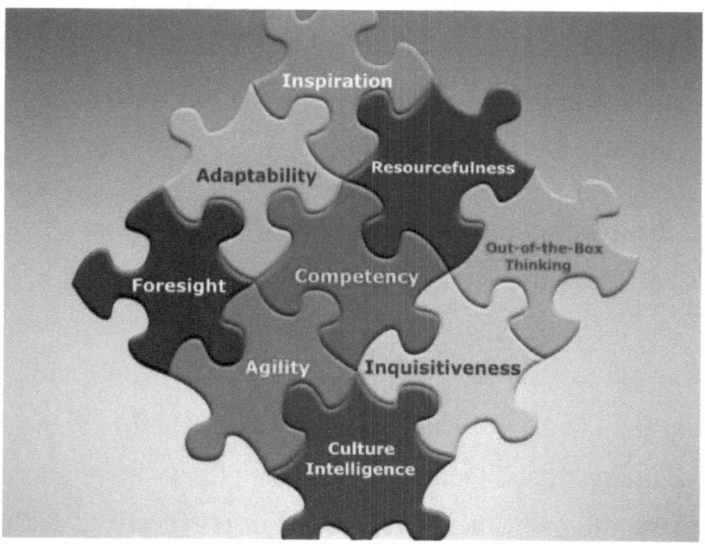

Figure 7 Nine Aspects of Creative Leadership

Creative leadership is the ability to inspire, to create, and to maintain the social and psychological conditions and the environment in which everyone is able to reach his or her highest potential; and contribute "leadership" in areas of his or her unique competencies.

- **Foresight:** Creative leaders are futuristic and forward thinking. Realizing that what has worked in the past isn't today's best solution and having the vision to see what it has now become. Creative leaders are the ones, who are capable of predicting future trends, manage the presence and delegate the past. In each context, a creative leader is always conscious of the changes needed to connect the past with the future, prospecting and communicating tangible such as resources and intangible such as cultural changes and identifying the proper vision for each cycle in the life of a corporation.

- **Adaptability:** Creative leaders are adaptable. Creative leadership is being flexible enough to adapt to the situation and the players involved. It means doing unexpected, unconventional things or methods to connect with your team - whatever it takes to get the job done, done well, and leaving everyone feeling good about it. It is similar to the situational leadership, where the leader has the flexibility and adaptability to use the wide range of leadership skills available to them and have the self-awareness to know when and how to use and develop the skills of those that they lead.

- **Inspiration:** Creative leaders are inspirational and motivational. Creative Leadership is when you think, act and enable others with a creative spirit that drives positive change. Creative leaders are those who will be able and capable of leading the entire management team by increasing their productivity, encouragement, capacity building, motivation, rewarding and appreciation, beyond their performances and open minded as well as friendly with the staff in the working field and able to get the hearts of staffs.

- **Resourcefulness:** Creative leaders are resourceful. Creative leadership is essentially anchored on the leader's overall multifaceted resourcefulness. That is, the multidimensional (including introspection) competencies to formulate creative (unconventional) alternatives or solutions to resolve problems, to show versatility and flexibility in response to unpredictable or unanticipated circumstances.

- **Out-of-the-box thinking:** Creative leaders are out of the box thinkers who can think outside the box, go against the grain; and at times throw away conventional means and try something radically new. Creative leadership is simply the capacity to think and act beyond the boundaries that limit one's effectiveness. Every leader or organization faces obstacles that are difficult to surmount - from corporate executives confronting the complex global marketplace to educators trying to lift student achievement to nonprofit groups and government agencies addressing critical social issues with tight budgets.

- **Inquisitiveness**: Creative leaders are inquisitive. The creative leader's mind starts from the very beginning, asks the fundamental questions such as,'why,' 'why not,' 'alternatives,' ''who,' 'who for,' and 'what are your learning experiences?' and then follow the courageous routes these questions take you, being prepared to stumble on the way. One aspect of genuinely Creative Leadership and that is the willingness to take risks - to break the rules, to push the envelope, to go beyond what is expected, and to deliver above and beyond the call of duty.

- **Competency:** The more "creative leaders" we have, the better for the world. The proper function, the ultimate criterion of "creative leadership," is the ability to create more leaders, to spread leadership - or, more precisely, to groom "followers" (the people for whom one is responsible) into leaders. Stated differently, "creative leadership" is the ability to develop the people for whom one is responsible into leaders in their own right.
  (1) Every human being, by reason of his or her uniqueness, has the potential to "lead" in one or more areas for which he or she is specially "equipped."
  (2) Some of the social and psychological problems that are afflicting individuals, institutions, and organizations might be due to inadequate opportunities for people to realize their potential and to contribute leadership in areas of their special competence; and, resultantly, personal sense of futility.

- **Culture intelligence**: Cognizance, sensitization, and sophistication to what cultural differences in leadership perceptions, approaches, and communications can contribute to our understanding of leadership, and what we deem as 'creativity' in leadership, which at times is down to cultural difference in traditions, practices and perceptions of organizational productivity and community 'norm.'

- **Agility**: Creative leadership can be described as "Adaptability meets Agility." Creative leadership is the unique combination of leadership behaviors that develops and achieves high quality and meaningful results over a sustained period of time. Creative leadership does this by challenging him/herself and staff to find optimal high-value solutions to provide clarity on high priority objectives, criteria, quality and results integrated with a strong expectation that innovative solutions can be found by engaging and challenging staff and partners to develop innovative alternatives. Take the team and sort of rearranging the chairs by assigning each to something new to them, reverse team roles, turn things upside down and approach problems from a 45-degree angle. Creative leadership requires the strength to review a recommendation for a problem or decision and reject it because the leader knows there has to be a better solution. This is done by challenging individuals and groups to think broader and deeper within the parameters of defined success criteria. As a result, a high achieving culture is built within an organization. It is the consistent expectation for innovative solutions while leading people to grow beyond existing levels of performance and capability. It combines restless dissatisfaction with the current state coupled with the excitement of leading individuals or groups to find solutions that will produce results no one thought possible.

The characteristics of genuine Creative Leadership show the following dispositions: Visionary, practical, adaptable, persevering, competent, ethical, courageous, and curious. These traits are supported by the following habits: Open minded, collecting thoughts and ideas, seeking new experiences, being playful, challenging the status quo, surrounding by interesting people, things, and environment, and enjoying solitude.

5 Three Traits of Innovative Team

Innovation journey is like taking a hiking trip on the trail very few or even no people ever went before, it takes courage and emotional maturity.

Due to the complexity of today's business dynamic, more often than not, innovation is teamwork, rather than just an individual's effort. What are the successful traits of an innovative team, and how to improve the team's innovation fluency?

- **Innovation leadership**: Innovation leadership is crucial, as leaders must have a clear vision and be strong in communicating it. An innovation leader must walk the tightrope between diplomat and maverick. An innovation manager is like an entrepreneur, but even has a more challenging job; an entrepreneur is a decision maker who always depends on his/her thought; decides what, how, and how much of a good work or service will be produced. He or she supplies risk capital as a risk taker, monitors and controls the business' activities as a manager. The success of innovation depends on proper management. Through proper management, the business is able to overcome the obstacles to managing successful innovations. An innovation leader may have his/her own constitutional innovation leadership behaviors across the innovation spectrum, as a creator, translator, stabilizer, or navigator, etc, with the pattern of required behaviors to face the emerging situation and succeed. The leaders in innovation today are problem-solvers, who have to create, manage, and orchestrate the innovation symphony not completely written yet; it takes practice, practice, practice.

- **Mutual trust:** If innovation starts with a vision, it's primarily a journey through which the innovator has to interact with others upon how to innovate; if you don't trust inputs from others, how do you innovate? Many good ideas get buried simply because the innovator fails in interesting others or in adapting to their input. Mutual trust presents openly to others and doesn't worry too much about hidden agendas. If you get enough feedback, unfair input should be easily identified; or it's not as simple as the case that once you phrase your vision, others will simply take it and transform it. Mutual trust is the prerequisite for creating innovation team harmony. In most cases of disagreement, it is ideological, such as the confused definitions, or how individuals process information that causes disharmony. Through trusting each other, the team can create synergy by understanding problems more profoundly and solving innovation puzzles more collaboratively.

- **Emotional maturity:** Innovation journey is like taking a hiking trip on the trail very few or even no people ever went before. It takes courage and emotional maturity. No matter if one is managing or participating in a collaborative environment, one's emotional maturity enables the suspension of judgment. The self-actualized individual proposed by Maslow's hierarchy of needs was able to clearly understand their perspective and try to understand and incorporate the understanding of others without feeling the egos cry for attention. It is both trust and emotional maturity (a highly self-actualized nature) that allow one to collaborate and easily integrate the ideas of others. Having clear constraints also improves the innovative environment. Innovators are the round pit, doesn't fit the square hole, they are disruptive to the status quo. But working with individuals who have a strong sense of self has many benefits as well. People tend to trust them because they say what they mean and mean what they say. Indeed, innovation is all about how to disrupt the outdated thinking and old ways to do things, sometimes it is emotional, but it's also a progressive and mature way to move forward.

Organizations need to invest in the cultivation of capacity for innovation. Mutual trust, innovation leadership, and emotional maturity are all critical to building highly effective innovation teams to achieve exceptional results.

6 Can Employees Learn to Be Innovative?

Innovation is to connect the dots - synthesizing that goes in one mind, and teamwork through collective insight.

Innovation is the light every forward-looking organization is pursuing; however, the business's innovative capability depends on its people, the team of talent who can transform the novel idea to achieve their commercial value. How should organizations train their staff to become more creative? And can employees learn to be innovative?

- **The perspective comes down to how you define innovation:** What one man calls innovation, another will say it is a trivial and self-evident step. What one person calls an act of genius, another will treat as unworkable insanity. The right kind of mind is the essential feature of real innovation. Those flashes of inspiration we now see in retrospect as groundbreaking inventions or innovations were driven by people not only far-sighted but determined to make their ideas succeed. Generally speaking, innovation actions, processes, and tools can be taught to employees. But innovation essentials, if you mean technical creativity, originality, insight, ingenuity, etc, can't be taught, but needs to be discovered by talent people on their own. History teaches that those gifted with ingenuity don't need stimulating; while those without it are barren ground when it comes to original thinking. If you are wired the right way you can recognize groundbreaking approaches and move ahead. It's not an ability you can impose by instruction, and no amount of examples, algorithms, lateral thinking guides or random approaches or methods will beat the 'synthesizing that goes on in one mind.'

- **Cultivating the culture of innovation is more important than training, in order to sow innovation seeds in organizations:** Ultimately, if the company doesn't have "the expectation of innovativeness" in its DNA, innovation training is all for naught. Better you create an atmosphere where staffs are encouraged to offer innovative, creative and insightful proposals for new products, new initiatives in cost reductions and better. Engagement by staff is increased when they are aware that there is a way to contribute; the innovative mind is often suppressed by the culture which discourages anything other than executive decision making.

- **Innovation in the context of large organizations, there is no choice but to enforce cross-functional communication and collaboration:** In businesses, especially the mature, large corporations and within that environment, innovations can range from small to game changers. Also, it is important to note that within the organizations, innovation is rarely an individual action; rather it is a team effort, often across multiple organizational silos. The flip side is the members of a team must always go the same way, and too often this is towards orthodoxy rather than innovation. Still, in the organizations which are huge and complex, even the ultimate innovator needs to build a coalition of support to get anything done within such an environment.

- **Innovation training isn't as simple as yet another training program:** If innovation is beyond ideas, then it becomes a little trickier to train, because it involves process, networking, empathy to others, tenacity, alliance, and drive to see innovation commercialized. All the methods and techniques in the world won't eliminate human nature. You're asking people to feel comfortable with the unknown. That takes time, those able to see further see further. Those able to take an ingenious path will do so given the opportunity. There are bound to be those with a latent ability who are never stimulated into proposing a 'solution' but have the ability. They come out of the woodwork at the moment you least expect.

- **The innovation training is also not one size fits all**: It shall not apply to every employee within an organization in the same format, but there is a broad range of individuals who can benefit from learning the skills of innovation, for themselves and for the broader organization. There is likely a sliding scale of innovation, where you have the total alpha innovators, there is much talk these days of intrapreneurs - the entrepreneurs within organizations, and then those who are somewhat innovative, and innovation programs are working hard to identify, support and leverage the skills of these individuals, so that they can add value. This is where a robust training program can not only give people new skills, but also make them feel engaged, increase their networks across the organization, and give them an opportunity to build the ideas that they are thinking of.

Thereof, innovation methodology, process, and tools can be taught. However, the innovation capabilities cannot be imposed by instruction or example. It is the nature of talent which should be discovered on their own, and nurtured through the teamwork. The organization's "Innovativeness DNA"- the culture of innovation is more critical than training, as fertilized soil to grow innovation fruit trees.

7 Design Thinking: A Useful Myth

The design does need more recognition as thinking and problem-solving process, maybe even a strategic differentiator.

Before it acquired a name, design thinking started as a rare activity that exceptional individuals did, it wasn't documented as a way of thinking, and it was completely mysterious to most others. Today, rather than being a mythological trend, the invention and popularization of the term "design thinking" reflect the emergence of an accessible thought framework, a holistic, flexible and creative way of seeing that anyone can appropriate - more than a specific set of codified methodologies. So, how to debunk such a popular myth –Design Thinking (DT)?

- **Non-linear thinking**: At its core, Design Thinking is NOT linear; it is NOT the kind of thinking that got you into whatever mess you're in the first place, it is NOT dedicated to perpetuating the status quo, it is NOT predicated on following a method. There are different tools and ways which you may or may not use to bang away at the issues, but as soon as you start assigning rules and processes, you are back to linear thinking - but with frills.

- **Outside-in view**: One of the great advantages of design thinking is to have the outside-in view, in most situations where the process isn't producing solutions. The "methodologies" being put into the design thinking bucket are somewhat unique and previously outside of the business norm, but have the potential to reframe the problem which in itself is a pretty huge contribution. You don't do certain things in a certain order; you just look at things from a non-business-standard point of view until the form emerges. Design thinkers aren't afraid to turn things inside out, look at them from underneath, break them down into bits and pieces, paint them purple and orange, shove bit A into bit B, all with no particular expectation that anything defined will happen, but it might be something else and that may push you in a useful direction.

- **Loosen-up**: Design thinking as a methodology, intends to loosen-up business planning process (writing product/market strategy documents with profit projections) and legitimize less regimented tactics, open to a multitude of inputs and influences. Traditionally, business people equal creativity with chaos and overlook the potential for solving problems the way designers work - starting with little certainty and heading for the unknown. The recognition that some transfer of approach is valid and actually provide structure to guesswork is not entirely an unrealistic proposition. Solving problems shares a lot of ground, irrespective of different professional domains. The increasing popularity of this meme implies a mind-shift in our cultural thought patterns which is creating a receptive and fertile field for the concept and actually frequently jars something loose in the brain that turns out to be a useful datum.

- **Start with the end in mind**: While doing actual work using Design Thinking, you must end with solutions, but you do need to understand that those solutions may come through back doors and side windows, or have perhaps been hiding in the basement. Therefore, always be careful in examining the potential points of engagement, rather than saying "first we'll fix this." Frankly, it can be a bit exhausting to explain the approaches to someone to whom such thinking is entirely alien, but it is necessary (usually). A sense of ongoing motivation needs the support of a notion that one has a hypothesis, appropriate skills, and tools. Often, the framework is simply a vocabulary of terms ascribed to the agency and a set of prescribed activities to formalize work.

A powerful myth has arisen upon the land, design thinking a myth that permeates business and academia, it is pervasive and persuasive. Design thinking is a practice; it takes a fairly uncommon interdisciplinary personality type to be interested in this approach. So at least in the short term, its usage will still probably remain in the hands of a relatively small group of professionals. But as going forward towards more radical digital transformation, the design does need more recognition as thinking and problem-solving process... maybe even a strategic differentiator. The trend globally will be toward interdisciplinary and systems-based design thinking.

8 Why 'Good Managers' are not always Good for Innovation

It takes an innovative adventure to grow a leader from good to great.

Modern managers are pillars of running complex businesses; good managers are disciplined, dedicated and accountable. However, in many cases, why are good managers not always good for innovation? What're the issues that stifle the development of innovation leadership? And how to flex innovation muscles in the management team?

- **Only follow the best practice, not contemplate the next practice:** 'Good managers' are the ones who try to stay on the straight and narrow, follow the experience and industry best practices to make the job done, lack a sense of adventure, and with the "it's just a job" mentality. Good managers use the tested and proven methodology and are least likely to deviate; they do things the same way they have been done, ALWAYS. To be a good innovator, one must be able to understand current situation via different lenses. Think out of the box to come up with a better way of doing the right thing. It's a different competency for which companies have to train and coach their managers.

- **Too much emphasis on control, not on enabling:** Is it because good managers are good because they always ensure they do the right thing right and their main concerns are to manage the team, processes and achieve their KPIs. They may put too much emphasis on controlling, not enough energy on innovation and unleashing talent potential.

- **Leverage innovation-enabling process and system**: If there is no support system put in place in some cases, managers are punished with the bad rating for not demonstrating an innovative streak when they didn't know that they were allowed to do so, let alone put it into practice. An innovation support processes or systems can be seen in companies which clearly indicate innovation as a required competency for managers, and it's tied to performance management and total reward system.

- **Lack of culture of failure tolerance:** To innovate you need to think differently from the rest, but in many traditional organizations, creative managers always get into trouble since they try new ideas which they hope will work. When these ideas do work, they get praise; and when they don't, they get 100% blame. It is caused by a lack of a culture of failure-tolerance. Start with personal awareness and change of mindset. An innovative leader will spend more time on contemplating the new possibilities, challenge the "we always do things like that" mindset, craft the next innovation practices, break down the silo processes and instill the openness and inclusiveness in the corporate culture.

- **Refine the reputation of being good managers**: Who are the good managers? A clear communication of what is expected of good managers and support system in cultivating the culture of innovation is crucial, as managers may be afraid to be innovative for the fear of failure alone. In a much simpler context, the manager should take it upon himself or herself to discuss innovative ideas with his or her superior who will mentor him or her in the implementation of the new ideas, whatever that may be. So it takes clear communication and talent management process with innovation as the expectation to be a good manager.

Being a good manager is not enough, being an innovative manager is even tougher. Being innovative is a state of mind, it is more critical than doing innovation. From good to great, it takes courage, creativity, insight, and discipline for effective managers to make an influence on the organization and society as well.

9 Is Innovator 'Trouble Maker' or 'Rain Maker'?

Innovators think different from non-linear or different angles.

Although innovation is the light every forward-look organization is pursuing, very few businesses have systematic approaches to managing it, or lack of a wise eye to recognize their special breed of talent - the innovators; or even worse, when innovator are punished for their initiatives, typically always "are you a troublemaker?"

- **Being a troublemaker is not a bad thing when it comes to innovating**: Innovation is all about doing something in such a way that gets noticed in a manner that disrupts legacy thinking or the old way to do things. In order for something to move, it may need to surrender first. So, true innovation always spurs certain disruption otherwise it is not innovation. People don't know how to react in front of something new, in front of something unknown. The feeling of fighting on the front line is unique; all the innovators experience that especially when they fight for their products and succeed.

- **Focusing on communicating insight is the key to restore innovation:** Innovation always appears with a strange cover. Communication problems are normal when something is new. When people can't formulate their insight with enough precision and they can't communicate that insight effectively and objectively, then the world is full of "trouble" makers; when innovative ideas get the right management support through the streamlined process, to transform into the new products/services/processes, or the innovators stimulate or foster the culture of innovation, and then innovators also become rainmakers.

- **Systematic innovation management can improve innovation success rate**: New ideas always cause troubles and it has a very low ratio to bring success. In such a case, people may feel pessimistic about how many chances the idea turns into innovation. That's why they resist new ideas - always troubles and doubts of success. Reduce the failure ratio and maybe the situation will change. Organizations should ideally have a sustainable approach to innovation. Systematic innovation methods can reduce the failure ratio down to accepted level; a systematic approach is to depict innovation as a system (rather than a traditional process) whose performance depends on the alignment of its various components (people, actions, controls, resources, etc.).

- **Innovators think differently from non-linear or different angles**: Innovators whose work continues to move forward and, in turn, is profitable to self and others think differently than those who are traditional thinkers. They see the old problems from every direction and find different solutions. However, the 'trouble' maker reputation is due to the lack of true democracy in most of the working places. This is unfortunate because such an old system needs innovators more than ever because they will break the chains.

- **The power of innovation may also come from the collective creativity and collaborative effort:** Have the good sense and charisma to attract or to surround yourself with the right people who can move the idea into action. Sometimes the main trouble is that every person follows his/her own interests, which coincide with the interests of the others' interests and the interests of the whole system. More often, innovation is a team effort, a group of 'troublemakers' may have to be fine-tuned to create synergy in making innovation fruitful.

Innovators are among us and within us, spot them on how they think and do things differently. Innovators are the ones who can see things differently, not negatively; dare to take risks, not risk-reverse; be 'disobedient' with good reasons. Empower them to build the culture of innovation. Encourage people to be creative, foster a creative environment in which people can unlock their creativity, to push the world forward, not backward.

Chapter 4

Connecting Innovation Dots

Innovation is the light every organization is pursuing. Innovation takes the cycle of observing-questioning-connecting- networking-experimenting.

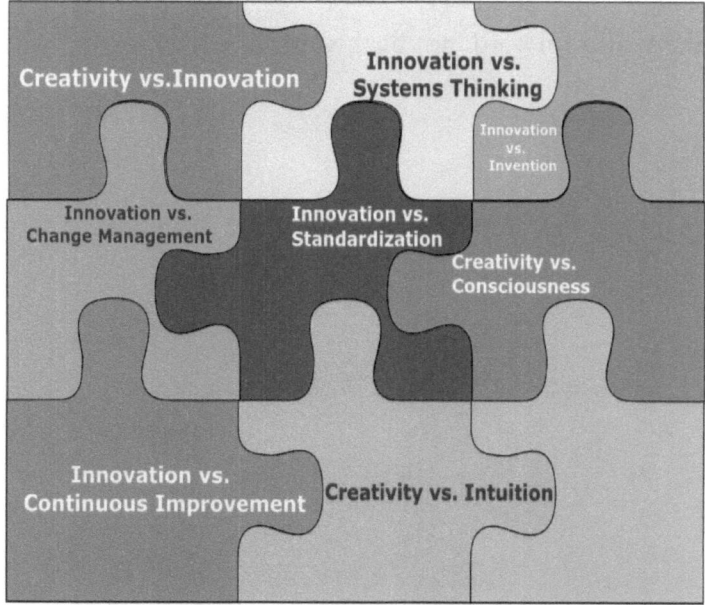

Figure 8 Connecting Innovation Dots

We all know innovation is important because it is the lifeblood of any business. Innovation is the light every organization is pursuing. Innovation takes the cycle of observing-questioning-connecting- networking-experimenting. From management perspective, innovation is essentially about reducing the unnecessary business complexity to tackle the complexities of business dynamic due to the hyper-complexity of modern businesses.

Innovation has more enriched context today than ever. Innovation is the process that transforms novel idea or knowledge into business value. The output from the process is the innovation. The exercise of deciding just what innovation is within each organization is the single most critical activity of an innovation effort. Because how an organization orchestrates to generate ideas, manages the activities, measures the results, etc, is determined by how that organization has decided to craft the innovation effort. There are many areas within a company where the innovation process can be applied to create value, from communication innovation to culture innovation, from process innovation to business model innovation; from product innovation to service innovation, the innovation context goes beyond the traditional scope. Here is a set of "dot-connecting" practices to enhance understanding of innovation management.

1 Creativity vs. Innovation

Creativity is the ability to create novel value, and innovation is how to transform ideas and achieve their business value.

Creativity is infused with an inner cohesion and comes from a vision of uniqueness. Creativity needs a problem, and a creative person needs a purpose. Innovation is to reinvent business, but not to reinvent the wheels. Innovation is about reinventing the business direction and purpose at any time. It defines strategy, profitability and relevance at any given time. If you do not innovate, you become commoditized and just like so many others who offer the same product or service. Innovation allows one to stand out and above the rest. The difference between innovation and creativity is implementation. One of the good definitions of innovation is: **"to transform the novel ideas into commercially successful products and achieving its business values."**

- **Creativity is the ability to solve, or attempt to solve problems:** Creativity is a mental process which results in an action that tests a possible solution. Things either work or they do not. That action is creativity. Creativity has two parts: the spark of inspiration (1st thought) which plants a new concept in our heads, and then the building of a structure of associations and relationships between that "seed" concept, and the many concepts already stored in our heads. The associations and relationships are what turn the spark into an expressible idea, and if we are lucky a useful idea. The initial spark only comes after your brain has toiled with the problem. Your subconscious brain loves creating solutions to problems that plague your conscious brain. Anytime an idea "pops" into your head, you have your subconscious to thank. Very rarely can you power your way through a problem using purely conscious thought. Thin-slicing refers to the fraction of a second between when you're confronted with a problem and when your subconscious knows the answer. Sometimes your conscious knows as well, other times you just get a feeling something is right or wrong.

- **Innovation is to transform novel ideas to achieve their business value:** It is very important to recognize that innovation is an essential factor for a company success. "Out of the box" thinking is the base for innovation that was very well said by Albert Szent-Györgyi (Nobel Prize Laureate), **"Research is to see what everybody else has seen, and to think what nobody else has thought."** One of the problems is how to manage the different cultures needed to do both things well in a mature organization and getting innovation capability embedded as an organizational capability. One of the issues in a lot of organizations is that the "innovation" part is often separate and a lot smaller than "business as usual," and so the culture of the larger part (via its leadership) is the one that wins the day.

- **Most of the organizations need both: the "into the box" and "out of the box" thinking:** The variety of research shows that 70 to 80% of successful innovations are based on "into the box" thinking. Most of the organizations need both: Out of the box and in the box/core innovation. Typically, the majority of projects come from the latter. How to accomplish this balance is a crucial issue for organizations. Shaping a bigger box by making connections between different boxes; rather than thinking outside of one particular box. Look at what other people have in their boxes, find out how their ideas different from what's in your box, and then think about what new structures can be built in space not yet occupied by anyone's box.

Building a creative working environment is, by nature, a cultural change. The creative work place is based on a triangle with three vertices: culture, method, and people. The ability of an organization to establish the right set of teams or people, collaboration and communication process that will eventually lead to innovation is the key.

2 Innovation vs. Change Management

Innovation is the optimal change; it cannot be successful without grounding change management.

Innovation is value creation in a different way or to a different element of the business; there are both disruptive innovation and incremental innovation. So, is innovation just another word for change; or does innovation management align with change management? Change and innovation share a common DNA, which is 'change' nature. But they are still different; each one has different motivators and must be managed differently. Innovation is a collection of thoughts, ideas, or efforts used to bring about or manage change to a desirable outcome. Not all change management is innovative; however, innovation only exists to bring about change. Innovations do not need to be new; however, they should at the very least implement an existing method, idea, or resource in a new way, thereby making it innovative to the particular challenge at hand.

- **Innovation is to "make meaningful connections":** Innovation can be delivered in many different ways. Organizations define what innovation means to them and how they choose or need to deliver, such as business model innovation, culture innovation, structure innovation, products/service/process innovation, etc. Change Management is not necessarily about innovation and an organization has to carefully evaluate what is working and what it wants to change. It must also consider not only the intended changes but what could be the unintended changes. Substantial innovations also sometimes lead to unexpected organizational changes, sometimes to handle success and sometimes to build on that success.

- **Innovation is a unique differentiator and a subset of change:** Innovation and change are not the same. The significant innovations can catalyze organizational change. Innovation has its own change dynamics, technically and organizationally. When change management is aligning with innovation, internally and externally, and that change can be part of innovation dynamics. Innovation always means change, but not all change is innovation. Managing innovation requires you as a leader, formal or informal, to shepherd an idea through several phases of development, knowing when to move forward and when to return to an earlier phase. Change management usually means moving a team or organization in a forward direction - successfully or not.

- **To be innovative requires a changeable mindset:** There is a willingness to "not know" and be able to source possibilities in the emergence space; be curious and receptive to improvisation and experimentation (and failing) and about how to maximize diversity, to be collaborative, and to intentionally disruptive to create the empty space to generate ideation, new ideas and solutions that we can be provocative, passionate (really intrinsically motivated) about and courageous enough to implement or execute in new and unexpected ways, from letting go of the current reality to allowing an unknown future state to emerge.

- **Innovation requires a much deeper whole system, an emergent, generative, iterative and integrative approach:** It requires much more time, energy, passion, courage, experimentation, retreat and reflection to get clear and focused on the innovative idea, business model, process or solution, and to then enact, embody and execute in a disciplined way. But both change and innovative leadership suggest that to deal effectively with change (their fears and resistance to it), businesses need to become good at self-managing, being adaptive, humanistic, and demonstrate flexibility and acceptance, to move and lead from current reality to desired future state.

You can't do innovation management successfully without grounding in change management. In the final phase of innovation, where the idea is evaluated, applied, adapted, and optimized, change management is essential, so that individuals and organizations can benefit from the value of the innovation. The common change management issues such as dealing with resistance should be considered throughout the innovation process; many issues related to adaptation of innovation can be predicted and managed by the way stakeholders are engaged in the process or journey of innovation. And, many change management processes will benefit from an innovative mindset and this can lead to practical, value-creating results.

3 Innovation vs. Continuous Improvement

Both innovation and continuous improvement are the way to adapt to changes; either stepwise, or breakthrough.

Innovation is the larger umbrella term that encompasses continuous improvement, innovation is also expanding its horizon, goes beyond products/services innovation, and it could mean business model/process/culture/leadership innovation as well. They are either the same or different in many ways.

- **Linear vs. nonlinear process**: Continuous improvement is a linear process pointed at creating stable processes. Innovation is a nonlinear process involving non-stable processes; continuous improvement expresses a stepwise process toward something "better," where the objective of the improvement can be anything and "better" can have just an internal meaning while innovation stands more for a project type of activity where the reference point could be business eco-system.

- **Different twist vs. old fashion way:** Innovation is happening when you change the game; you bring a different twist to what is currently established and perceived. Continuous improvement is by tweaks of things in the old fashion way to bring efficiency. But, even a very small improvement leveraging a new way of doing things, bringing an outside method, or view, shifting the paradigm, is innovation. Innovation breakthroughs that really hit the spot are nearly always
  (1) respond to a true human need;
  (2) ride on emerging trends;
  (3) simplify business models;
  (4) combine all the firm's capabilities in a unique way to
   (a) wow customers and,

(b) build entry barriers.

- **Specialty vs. transdisciplinarity:** Continuous improvement takes specialty; while innovation is trans-disciplinary. Continuous improvement = technical specialists making the product/service more efficient, up-to-date to the consumer needs. Innovation happens when a non-specialist question challenges the rules of the game, invents knowledge transfers and goes outside the industry to invent a radical new way to respond to the 'job to be done.' It can also be categorized into

  (1) Intersection innovation, that is, ideas that result from the clash of consumers and producers are more likely to be out of the box and disruptive, more readily identifiable as innovation.

  (2) Directional innovation that results from either the producer or consumer is more likely to resemble continuous improvement.

- **Improvement- innovation as a continuum:** Innovation can be defined as a continuum, with smaller improvements being closer to one edge (the incremental one) and radical changes being the other edge. In any case, the "newness" of any change in question is relative and depends on which dimension of change one chooses.

  (1) Continuous Improvement - you take a base and build upon it.

  (2) Innovation - you build off an entirely new base. Also, in innovation, you find new ways to expand the market to beyond the people already involved.

- **Incremental innovation vs. radical innovation:** It may be easy to split the term "innovation" into two categories: "incremental innovation" and "radical innovation."
  (1) Incremental innovation has equal notion/concept with continuous improvement, focusing on improving a part of business process.
  (2) Radical innovation focuses to "replace" conventional value stream with a new one, supported and filled with noble knowledge and idea. "If at first an idea is not absurd, there is no hope for it." Einstein was obviously holding out for disruptive change.

- **The scope, scale and impact of the changes:** The broader the scope, scale, and impact of the change, the more one leans towards calling such change an innovation. Some additional variables that might merit consideration are the scope, scale, and impact of the change. Two key factors are
  (i) the impact on the corporation;
  (ii) whether there is increased revenue generation, either from expanding existing markets or creating entirely new markets.

The very successful organizations must manage a portfolio of initiatives, prioritized with adequate support, across the whole spectrum; make the current business better; look for new business and everything in between.

- **Innovation is "a change that adds stakeholder value":** Now if your stakeholders are internal process owners and your output stakeholders are the same, the type of innovation you have is Continuous Innovation. If you take knowledge from one context and bring it over into a new context, and you have knowledge or technology transfer innovation. With continuous process improvements, you often reduce costs and increase productivity without increased revenue generation. On the other hand, if the change, whether an improvement on an existing process or the addition of an entirely new process, leads to increased revenue generation, either from the expansion of an existing market or the creation of a new market, then it's more as innovation.

The purpose of concept differentiation is not about separating and siloing these changes but how to best link them together, focus on core activities on innovation - having a suite of tools and people to help realize the change you have defined. Innovation needs to be introduced all over the spectrum of the product lifecycle (refreshing the portfolio, finding totally new fields or ensuring on-going profitability and extension of the current portfolio). An organization must also seek continuous improvements all the time, with a combination of introducing tweaks and innovations.

4 Innovation vs. Systems Thinking

The foundation for innovation has to be grounded in the "vision" which is linked to "hope" and seeking justice or "truth."

For many organizations, innovations are still serendipitous. However, serendipity can be planned into a management discipline. Serendipity is not a lucky accident; it can be planned and worked upon. Creativity is all about connecting the dots; Systems Thinking is about how to discover the patterns underlying these dots, to understand the relationship between parts and the whole. How can we dig through the innovation from Systems Thinking perspective though?

- **Creativity and innovation lead us to understand "self" and wholeness:** Since innovation, the practical application of creativity is essentially about problem-solving at various levels, and to solve a problem implies a wish to make something, or everything perfect. That, in itself, seems to lead to a wish for understanding the wholeness. The interaction between what is within us (the Self), and how we project to the exterior world is the bridge to achieving wholeness. The constant negotiation between our essence and our projection is what leads to growth and human evolution. "Self" is that level of existence which is the genuine substance of who you are. It is eternal, yet it is unique to you. You are unrepeatable. In other words, you are the expression of the eternal "Self" in a singular way. You are the Self. Do you think the development of the "Self" is something that is well defined in most individuals at a young age or at all and does it take time, like wisdom from experiences in life for us to know the "Self"? The projection of "Self" to the exterior could mean that we try to change the "Self," or we try to change the exterior. The interaction between the Self/You and the exterior world which is a projection of you is Consciousness (with capital "C"), which is trying to manifest itself in a way that is unique to you. That is your unique gift. You are the light of knowledge and your light is also the goal of the universal knowledge. It is your light that is helping in sparking creativity and evolution of consciousness.

- **Innovation is an outcome of processes in the business ecosystem:** The foundation for innovation has to be grounded in the "vision." It has to be linked to "hope" and seeking justice or "truth." This causes conflicts because even though we might all have similar guideposts for our inner wholeness, we don't have the same grasp of truth unless we can accept the similar wholeness of our inner self. It is self-imposed by trying to make our "visions" reality. Just as we find energy is released from one steady state to another, we find innovation from our outer realities attempts to change to the steady state of our inner self. This energy is called innovation. Discovering the "truth" requires some analysis to understand multiple opinions and emotions which in many cases are among differing views and distorted facts, the inner and outer self is the struggle between what we know as reality and what we feel as our connection to the universe (wholeness within). The reality is the environment which is more in tune with the climate change, but inner wholeness is constant which relates to universal knowledge, and each of us has to find this constant for ourselves. We can help each other because it is the same truths for all humans, but to consume truths requires letting go of reality or setting aside the climate while we deliberate. This speaks volumes to customs and traditions that we humans have tried to mirror as "truths." However, the real truth is that they can change and the human race will continue to proceed. So, is innovation happening when we try to change the exterior, the environment outside ourselves? We look at people and people's activities, come to think of some possession or experiences which will make them related, send meaning to their life, or the meaning of their work, etc, make them see real value in terms of the investment they are ready to shell out for possession or experience of the same. That is a possibility to build a business around the idea or a concept arrived after meta-pattern recognition.

- **There is an emotion life cycle in an innovativeness process:** We seem to all be seeking what human emotions drive us to create or innovate. There is a pairing of emotions to many actions. We cannot have an action development without the psychological security (an emotion) and we cannot sustain security without development. The kind of emotions within a person that triggers an improvement/innovation process can be numerous and most likely will be a combination of emotions! Certainly when you think that every rational thought is linked to emotions and creates a feeling. This is an ongoing process just like the feeling to improve and to create. We may need conflict to initiate, but after initiation there should be a debate to create! So different kind of emotions is involved to truly become innovative. The conflict can come from an internal conflict or a conflict with the outside world. The most difficult part is to transform the conflict from within to a productive life cycle. This is wholeness. If you have a stable internal process and you can even help others, then innovation with the outside world will be the next challenge. The patience relates to tolerance and tolerance gives us the ability to understand other points of view; tenacity could help lead to your vision, and keep things on track etc. Stamina is perhaps a physical requirement to maintain this tenacity. However, innovation for the sake of innovating is exhaustive because what would be the purpose? The need to solve a problem might lead to innovation, but a need to innovate isn't addressing the problem. There are more situations related feelings that have an impact on you as a person or on your team. What about trust? Or what about happiness? So, your emotional well-being has an impact on innovation, but what is triggering your emotions? What from the outside world has an impact? What about the right innovation climate? Your personal climate, your team climate or your organizational climate? Historically, innovation would seem to have emerged with an instinct for survival. Basic tools for hunting and gathering. So there's a connection, with emotional equivalents, with surviving each day. Greater leaps are found with agriculturally based societies; whereas, nomadic groups seem to have remained static, having adapted through trading. Environment either encourages or discourages innovation, the ease or difficulties inherent in surviving.

Entrepreneurship begins with selling yourself and your value before any product is produced. Professionals as people do something because they enjoy or want to, not just for the money, but for the benefits it produces, the progress it achieves, and the satisfaction it gives us - the wholeness of self or the purpose of life. Money is important, but not an only motivation. Innovation is creating to improve a state (process, person, product etc). Improvement itself and the desire to improve come from within. Nowadays, with the speed of changes in the digital era, innovation is no longer a "nice to have," but a "must have" factor in the business success. Leveraging Systems Thinking in harnessing innovation is all about taking a scientific approach to problem identifying and solving. It allows you to master a number of things such as, embracing uncertainty, identifying interconnections and interdependencies, understanding flows or the lack of them, and identifying business opportunities, for ultimately, achieving innovation success.

5 Innovation vs. Invention

Innovation = f (Invention, Commercialization).

Innovation comes from the Latin, "Innovare" - 'to change or alter things that already exist.' Invention, on the other hand, has its roots in the Latin word "Novare," 'to make new/create.' Invention creates; innovation realizes value. Innovation is the practical application of new inventions into marketable products or services. Invention is making ideas from money; innovation is making money from ideas.

- **Invention creates, innovation applies creatively:** Innovation is the introduction of something new or the new way to do things. Invention is about something is invented as
  (1) a product of the imagination;
  (2) a device, contrivance, or process originated after study and experiment.
  Innovations = different and new. Invention = just new. Innovative ways of thinking lead to unique, value-added inventions or improvements to current inventions. So, innovation is more process driven and invention is more product oriented.

- **Invention precedes innovation, but innovation does not always need invention**: Innovation may or may not require an invention. If it does not require an invention, then it is incremental innovation; if it does require an invention, then it could be something like disruptive innovation, whatever that is! Invention is the origin, innovation is the destination. Invention =conceptualization to developing something new. Innovation =developing over the existing product to have better feature. Invention transforms challenges and problems into creative answers. Innovation is the integration of the invention into real world process, delivery system, market, and large-scale supply as well as combining the invention's technology into the other technology components (formulation) of the target product.

- **Invention is to create what does not exist; innovation is to improve what exists:** There is a fundamental problem with the comparison. Invention is a well-understood term at least legally as the novelty test is really black and white, but innovation is not. When do you have innovation? At what point is it achieved? Innovation is coming up with something of value by applying it to a product or process. The application is the invention. If invention is the creative storyline, innovation is the movie. Innovators are therefore, a complex mix of screenplay writers, casting agents, director, of course, production assistants, etc. And if they have cash, they may even be able to call themselves the producer!

- **Innovation = Invention + Execution**: Invention - creating new possibilities. Innovation - creating sustainable competitive advantages.

(1) What about the impact of innovation/invention dynamics on intangible dimensions of the output (services)?

(2) Tangible and intangible dimensions are almost always impacted together even if in different ways/different degrees. What about those combinations?

- **Innovation is the synthesis of invention and commercialization:** Innovation = f (Invention, Commercialization). It helps measure by:
(a) Identifying innovation by seeing invention density, and
(b) Integrating "audience recognition" to innovation, which clarifies measurement and suggests relativity.

- **Innovation is about having new knowledge and new processes:** Innovation is the specific phenomenon of the knowledge-based economy. Innovation is about too much knowledge in terms of too many good creative ideas, and too little available resources. Innovation is about prioritization - a system that can "smell" the right idea at the right time and place.

If invention is a picture snapshot, and then innovation is a colorful playbook, with all possible combinations of scenarios and all shades of relationships: Defining, distilling, determining, disrupting, potentiality vs. realization (in a context). Organizations just have to learn from experimenting, amplify the best practices, and build innovation as a core and differentiated business capability.

6 Innovation vs. Standardization

Raise your consciousness of the balance, and that, in and of itself, makes a world of difference.

Standards are a form of embodied technical knowledge accessible to all types of businesses that enable more effective product and process development. Innovation is how to transform novel ideas to achieve their business value. Innovation expands its horizon, to include soft innovations such as communication innovation or culture innovation; besides hard innovations such as product/service/business model/process innovations. Innovation vs. standardization: How to strike the right balance of innovation and standardization to run a successful business?

- **The strategy must take account both standardization and innovation:** There could be diverse levels of standardization. Usually, companies want standardization of internal reasoning (capitalization of previous experience, cost control, convenience, etc.). Also, companies are obliged by the external environment to be flexible (customers, suppliers, competitors). Strategies must take into account these two main poles:

- Profit through standardization (volume);
- Profit through innovation and flexibility (diversification).

- **A strategic approach to standardization and innovation must be done on two levels**:
  (a) At the new product; (b) At the processes of existing products. To improve efficiency in cost (low), then you need standardization. To become effective from the change (value perceived by customers), then you need innovation. However, the "dosage" of standardization and innovation in the new product is the key - meeting target costs (target costing process) in the product design phase (phase engineering) is the path worth following. Standardization 'versus' innovation can actually be standardization 'and' innovation. However, people in tactic or operational management usually face a hard time to understand that they actually can go hand-in-hand together in an appropriate way.

- **Standardization is inside-the-box (ITB); and innovation is outside-the-box (OTB)**: Some may equate outside-the-box (OTB) thinking with innovation, and similarly equate inside-the-box (ITB) thinking with standardization. Hence, organizations indeed need both, and in fact, cannot realistically exist without a healthy balance of both. That balance, ought to actually be strongly in favor of standardization at the vast majority of the time! Think 80:20 rule here, although the golden ratio may vary based on the culture, capability and overall maturity of the organization.

Consider the continuum between innovation and standardization. Business should always be open to, conscious of, and feel empowered to act upon-Out of box-OTB thinking. It is only when you reject the ability to "challenge conventional wisdom" (standardization) that ITB becomes problematic. It is very much a "consciousness" thing, imagine yourself rising above that continuum, and looking down upon the balance between the two. What you've just done is to raise your consciousness of that balance, and that, in and of itself, makes a world of difference. High mature organizations indeed need both, standardization and innovation, the matter is to figure out how and when to apply them in the most effective way.

7 Creativity vs. Consciousness

A combination of conscious and unconscious factors allows us to follow through our initial creative impulse.

All living beings are creative and we, humans, like to think that we are the most creative beings of all, not too sure about that. But speaking of humans, our creativity fluctuates, seems to disappear at times, get blocked, or sparkle in abundance and flow out of us some other times.

While an average adult gets about 70,000 random thoughts in a day, the brain can maintain only one thought at the same moment. So, what's the correlation between creativity and consciousness?

- **Creativity is coupled to consciousness through control:** Consciousness is the living being, and with its senses active and deliver something useful to itself or others. Creativity is a combination of something currently non-existent, thoughts, acts and with or without constraints. To be creative, you need to be conscious, curious about things that surround you. To be conscious is to be aware and engaged with both the inner world of thought, feeling, choice, and the exterior world of experience and relationship. The interaction between these two parts of our existence is the home of our creativity. It is the grist for our creative mill. It enables to connect seemingly unconnected items to build something new.

- **Creativity and consciousness are interlinked, like the two strands of the same DNA:** One cannot exist without the other. Creativity is born from conscious awareness and its complexity is given by the level of consciousness that is reached. Creativity is about listening to the silence for whatever wants to be revealed and expressed; emptying oneself from what is known, entering the unknown, trusting the mystery that invites us into a self-discovery journey that encompasses body-mind-heart-soul. Creativity is consciousness. It's such a desire that sends a true spark through, allowing one to see how all things can be both connected or disconnected to create completely new forms, systems, and ideas.

- **What fuels creativity? It is a combination of intrinsic and extrinsic factors**: On one hand, we have the level of curiosity, desire to learn and natural ability to maintain an open and inquisitive mind; and on the other hand, we have the conditions of the environment in which we operate, with all restrictions, needs, gaps, and pressures that might push our creative minds to soar. And then, of course, it is the ability to tap into the universal consciousness, a state of pure awareness where our mind is completely open to receive new ideas from the collective pool. Creativity comes into play when we call upon our conscious mind with the intention to bring forth solutions from our unconscious. As human beings, consciousness is at the heart of who we are. Our minds have access to both conscious thoughts and at times unconscious thought. It is a conscious mind we call with some unconscious activities of allowing creativity flow, as many creatives or inventors may tell you, ideas tend to come when you stop thinking about the problem, and they would also say it involves that allowing to be part of a process of trial and error. We all have this ability and it can be developed so we should encourage people, particularly young children to consciously use their creative imagination to create a better world.

- **Creativity is not a "thing," it´s a process that happens as a proactive mental activity to a problem:** Creativity is as much defined by the problem as by the capacity of the individual to connect things to resolve that problem in new and sometimes unexpected ways. The nature of consciousness is important in creativity. To be truly creative requires the suppression of many of the parts of our consciousness which we rely on most heavily in everyday life. If creativity is the process of assembling previously disparate or unconnected ideas into a new whole, then it can only be a conscious act to do so. That process may start with a 'what if' or 'if only' moment or a direct challenge to find a solution. Inspiration, on the other hand, may arrive from the unlikeliest of sources or disconnected thoughts and almost invariably when the conscious effort to be creative has been suspended.

- **Creativeness might also be the minds expansion into freedom:** Creativity involves birthing something into existence which was not there before. This involves consciousness of a high order. To the extent that spirituality encourages you to think beyond visible limits, it cannot help but aid in the creative birthing process. Creativeness derives from one's ability to let go. Let go of assumptions and stigmas we place on objects, ideas, function, and has a vision of purpose besides what is already obvious. The willingness to fail and try again in order to one day succeed. The creative people should have a high level of intelligence so that this longing can be converted to thought which has the capacity to explore unusual pathways. The person should have the capacity to enter into moments of reverie during which his/her frustrated thoughts, unanswered problems etc, reorder them and receive an insight. The creativity can be sparked by an epiphany or it might be a work in progress. Once we start to formulate an idea, it can lead us to make connections with other experiences we have had in our lives until we finally have a final product we are satisfied with.

A combination of conscious and unconscious factors allows us to follow through our initial creative impulse; idea generation process is also the capacity to focus. Focus gains clarity. Clarity increases awareness and awareness taps into new, creative and innovative views of the world.

8 Creativity vs. Intuition

Intuition is more about "gut feeling," and creativity is about "thinking-out-of-the-box."

The word intuition comes from Latin verb intueri which is usually translated as to look inside or to contemplate. According to the online dictionary, it is "the ability to understand something instinctively, without the need for conscious reasoning." Creativity is a person's innate ability to create novel ideas. Creativity is as much defined by the problem as by the capacity of the individual to connect things to resolve that problem in new and sometimes unexpected ways. What are the further correlations between creativity and intuition?

- **Intuition is about "thinking fast"; and to be creative, you need to be conscious and curious about surroundings:** Intuition is thus often conceived as a kind of inner perception, sometimes regarded as lucidity or understanding. Many may think intuition is opposite to logic, but more precisely, an intuitive mind is a complementary thinking process to rational thinking. So intuition is the quality or ability to have such direct perception or quick insight. It's a subconscious mode of evaluation that can help better understanding the so-called "reality," in which we operate, maximize our engagement with the broader and deeper aspects of our mind and our experience. Creativity is a combination of something currently non-existent, thoughts, acts and with or without constraints. To be creative, you need to be conscious, curious about things that surround you. To be conscious is to be aware and engaged with both the inner world of thought, feeling, choice, and the exterior world of experience and relationship. The interaction between these two parts of our existence is the home of our creativity.

- **Intuition is more about "gut feeling," and creativity is about "thinking-out-of-the-box"**: Intuition or being intuitive is when you have a gut feeling about something. It is when there isn't an exact answer to the puzzle because you don't have all the pieces. Chaos needs to be navigated by intuition. Intuition is also called gut-feeling; because it seems to have got to do something with the gut. Creativity is a result of living in your intuitive space. It is an action or a reaction to the world, from that place; it has no fear or traditions. It's not only about trying to "think outside the box," but an intuitive expression and alternative path that takes you wherever it needs to go, without boundaries. The fear or uneasiness is only the ego getting in the way. On the broadest level, creativity is embodied in the act of creating a self, through narrative, and this is the most fundamental creative effort we make. The big issue is that intuition needs some kind of catalyst - we need to be provoked to make our intuition work. Sometimes that can be as easy as asking a right-brain-oriented question. An intuition should be taken as a new insight, a new idea, a new angle, but must be backed with sound reasoning in the end before putting it into action. In this regard, intuition and creativity are converged.

- **Intuition is a deeper sense, and creativity is an innate process:** The research suggests that intuition, despite its flaws, is integral to our thinking. Intuition is a deeper sense which gets activated only if we are aligned with nature and the present. Some say it helps us make connections between events to understand a chaotic world, and others suggest it's necessary for us because we must have some immediate perception of events. Creativity is an innate process to create novel ideas. There's a critical link between creativity and intuition. An intuitive mind has the strength and the willpower to follow the courageous heart, and thus, having the better chance to be creative and creativity is more a process of flow. It starts somewhere, it is thought over, it is brought into relation and it is worked out; a process with a seemingly beginning and end. Creativity plays its part in all the steps.

When you are courageous enough to follow the gut, and curious enough to understand the surroundings, you learn how to liberate the imagination and come up with a new approach to the world. So, every person has the ability to be creative, just tearing down the mental barriers they have and tapping into their inherent abilities and enlighten the intuitive wisdom.

Chapter 5

Digital Innovation Next Practices

Innovation is the book never ends.

Figure 9 Digital Innovation Best and Next Practices

The world is becoming more hyper-connected with the latest digital technology advancement, are we ready to open the new chapter of digital innovation? Can we develop an approach which also places social, political and ethnic differences within a common framework to generate meaningful progress toward the next level of innovation? Is it possible to integrate the innovative concepts into a comprehensive approach that can generate intelligent solutions to the seemingly insurmountable large-scale problems? For example, how do you balance the partitioning of land and sea between man and nature? How can you use energy from sunlight to recycle all mass at the molecular scale locally? And if you were the Chief Innovation Officer in the organization or on the Earth, what's your innovation agenda?

- **Look uphill to identify the real problems**: Looking uphill can help to identify the real problems that matter, and on a scale that can make a difference. Looking deeply into the future can have a profound effect on where we go, and how we get there. From this perspective, both uphill and into the future, we gain an understanding of the unintended consequences of our actions in the future, and how to anticipate problems of our own making. Besides those macro, large-scale problems, at the intermediate or micro level, for either organization or individual, how do you get motivated to be innovative at daily basis via solving real-world problems large or small, in a creative way. Innovation is not for its own sake, but for problem-solving.

- **Think bigger:** It all starts at the beginning, to make the most impact. If we always do the same thing the same way, we'll always get the same result. What can we do differently? What is stopping people from being autonomous, pursuing mastery and seeking purpose? It's mastery by each individual when time permits and a singular purpose that involves the immediate reaction. This is part of the cognitive surplus. Yet, there are many who do not feel comfortable with self-direction, nor do they look to their jobs for the level of potential that is possible.

- **Motivation**: As a Chief innovation officer, you need to listen, convey, inspire, motivate, bring in people to share the vision, inspire the mission, communicate the ideas, advocate people-centricity, start with the project, fund it, listen some more, create your next wave of innovation gurus, creative communicators, savvy experts, community activists, and make smart investments. Asking them to look into the future should trigger their imaginations. And having a true consideration for life provides a bit of guidance on how and why we undertake these efforts. The lives of kids, life swimming in the ocean, lives of the birds and beasts, and life in the inner cities, all matters. We're dealing with the complexity of the whole planet. And if we're going to take action or promote behavior that we need to also assume responsibility for our advocacy.

- **Innovation Life Cycle Management:** Having solved the motivation problem, and moved out of the way, what do you think the nearly 7 billion people on the planet would do if they had more autonomy, mastery, and purpose? Or put another way, what're the best or next innovation practices, what is the structure for innovation? Money alone will not do it. Speakers or classes or signage or slogans will not do it. It requires acknowledgment, involvement, and commitment. It also needs to have principles, processes and performance measurement. Many like P-I-N approach to start handling new ideas:
P - What is POSITIVE about the idea?
I - What is INNOVATIVE about the idea?

N - What are the NEGATIVES, problems, risks?

Digital innovation has a broader spectrum with hybrid nature; it is the incremental improvement- radical innovation continuum. It is hard to think of any innovation as not a hybrid, a combination of something old with something new or a number of new things. Probably, the more hybrid, the old familiar things are combined, the less likely is any disruption, although all innovations are disruptive of something or some behavior to some degree. The innovation leaders need to master at managing complexity and building a healthy innovation portfolio effortlessly

1 What Triggers Innovation?

Innovation is a discipline that, if understood fully, reads more like a blueprint than science fiction.

The dictionary defines invention as 'a product of the imagination' and innovation as "the act or process of introducing new ideas, devices, or methods." Everyone has, at least, one good idea that is capable of invention and innovation, great or small, manifested by overcoming that inner fear. Innovation does not just accidentally happen; it can be managed in a systematic way. But first, you need to figure out: What triggers innovation?

- **The essence of innovation is made of trying new combinations of known things:** It's the essence of evolution. Each human being is a potential innovation by definition as you won't find two humans that are exactly the same. We are all new combinations of the known. The traits of innovation include:

  - simply about how some people can see what's around easily and discover a better way to do it effortlessly;

  -is capable of innovating if they are capable of silencing the noise in the mind and thinking outside the conditioned mind without fear;

  - nonlinear, parallel thinking and tangential thinking provide more opportunity for innovation than linear thinking;

  -What many see as innovation is actually problem-solving: a simple process of deduction to derive a solution drawing from knowledge, experience or a pool of data.

- **Knowledge and practices are relevant to innovation; doing more results in more opportunity for innovation:** Innovation comes with the increased knowledge and understanding of facts. You never know how innovative you might be in some field before encountering the problems and before the adoption of solutions. Innovators are often the individuals who are so passionate about their jobs that they live it on their own time (work related hobbies, testing theories, products, and applications) and they can focus better on what they are doing by diminishing distraction. If that kind of employee is working for you; not only do you have assurance, you are getting value for the compensation you are spending, you cannot help but get better results.

- **Innovation is a strategic choice**: If you want to be an "innovative organization," you shape your current business structure to match your current stack rank of areas where innovation will reap the most significant benefit. Innovation then happens in three ways - it enhances your core technology, it finds a better balance with adjacent technology, or it is completely new, which is transformative. Innovation isn't a magic word. Innovation is a discipline that, if practiced well and understood fully, reads more like a blueprint than science fiction. Innovation is only a strategic choice if you

are in possession of some "how-to"s. Believing it is possible for anyone is a necessary, but insufficient condition for successful execution. Giving people the "how-to"s makes all the difference. In addition, emphasizing that innovation is a journey enables people to pace themselves and recognize that innovation is not an on-off switch. There will be ups and downs along the way and you need the resilience to make the trip to completion. Innovation includes both breakthrough and incremental improvement. Improvement has two parts to it:
(1) Acceptance that perfection is impossible, that there's always room for improvement.
(2) a commitment to improvement followed by actions that implement improvement.

- **Brainstorming activates creativity which can be transformed into innovation:** The key to brainstorming is not to evaluate your ideas. Just let the ideas flow. Since most of the people have allowed themselves to get preprogrammed by the hidden hand in society and are only able to think along pre-programmed neural pathways. In order to think out-of-box and to "silence the noise of the mind," one needs to be involved in a menial task that does not require much of a conscious effort to execute, thus, allowing background operations to run such as brainstorming a solution to a problem. Innovation is all about the madness of solving problems and doing things in the newer way. So a few innovation traits include:

(1) Learn to forget (not use) what you have been "educated" in the past.

(2) Start using the other half brain for a change.

(3) Learn to trust and follow your gut feelings and capture insight.

Change is flow, and is necessary, but innovation should bring healthy, sustainable change with more pros than cons. People are all part of the Status Quo and it isn't until they are forced by circumstances that you change. You are driven to change and improve, as things change, the old paradigm becomes incompatible with the new reality and there occurs a digital paradigm shift, we will need to focus on innovation rather than over-specification. This may be very painful, but very helpful in a reassessment of what we stand for as a race.

2 What are the Best/Next Practices to Keep Innovation Alive in a Company?

Innovation is about moving forward. In any business, if you are not moving forward, you are moving backward.

Innovation is to transform novel ideas to achieve their business value. It is very important to recognize that innovation is an essential factor for a company's long-term success. However, becoming a truly innovative company is difficult, due to the risks involved and management skills needed. Some might complain innovation has distracted them from their strategic focus; the fact is that innovation is an important element of your business strategy, so the problem is how you can keep innovation alive in your organization?

- **Groom innovation leaders boldly:** Innovation is all around - the main problem is from the top accepting these ideas and respecting people's innovativeness. How would you assess profitability if you do not make a wholesome effort to innovate? There are nervous leaders in some organizations that refuse to innovate, use the same line of "profitable innovation" as an excuse. Eventually abandoning the effort to follow convention. To keep innovation alive in organizations, it is necessary first; assure your think tank that you are willing to make an investment with calculated risk.

- **Develop employees entrepreneurially:** Let them do things and solve problems in their own way to meet good results. Though the guide is needed at that crucial time, you will see innovations in your company' pipeline. Management should direct workflow, support the health of the team, create an environment where people want to work, encourage brainstorming. If management is successful, innovation will follow. Stop and re-model the company around the passions of the people within it; find the new stars and let them drive. Business innovation is bravery - it may take you to a whole other place.

- **Mind innovation gaps substantially**: The gap between the discovery-driven and delivery - driven management is critical and often leads to conflicts, deluding the transfer. When innovative skills and capabilities an organization always needs depend on the circumstances the business is in. Many companies form and grow on the basis of "idea creation," but then get bogged down when trying to "commercialize" those ideas - which require different skillset, focus, and even a needed passion.

And, if a company's focus swings too far to the commercialization side of the equation, then innovation suffers and vice-versa. Companies form a great technology, product or service concept, but when that initial innovation reaches end-of-life, there may not be an aptitude or capability present to continue generating a needed innovation cycle. If you can create a culture that nurtures creativity and innovation, you might be onto something. People will dare to be innovative as long as they know they won't get penalized for a bad idea, and may get rewarded for a good one. Priority, process and resource framework can be tools to manage innovation more effectively. If a company would like to stay ahead, it needs to preserve a commitment to the discovery-driven (Disruptive Innovation) path to ensure that they are pursuing blue ocean, do not end up in the red-ocean and gets too paralyzed (self-sustained) in its perfection of a business that has a wrong foothold business model.

- **Focus on long-term business prosperity**: Innovation comes with a risk of failure, usually not well tolerated in a market governed by risk-allergic mindset. Due to the nature of job duty, some works (entrepreneur, artist, engineer, etc.) are more creative; the other types of job are perhaps more compliant or calculative ("bean-counters"). We are what we think. Some mindsets are only concerned with quarterly ROIs and protecting passive shareholder equity to satisfy the preoccupations of investment capital. Innovation comes with a risk of failure, usually not well tolerated in a market governed by risk-allergic mindset. Still, when business leaders, regardless what type of mind you have, go beyond short-term gain, take a calculated risk and make a long-term investment, organizations have a better opportunity to shift from surviving to thriving mode.

Innovation is about moving forward. In any business, if you are not moving forward, you are moving backward. There is no standing still. Companies have to be prepared to lose some to gain more for the longer term. That's the mantra for you to keep innovation alive and thrive in your organization.

3 How to Build a Creative Workplace

Creativity is a "domain" contextualized competency.

In recent years, creativity has become a very highly valued skill. Creative people combine existing possibilities to reach more often unexpected solutions. Creativity is an essential building block for innovation in businesses. Everyone possesses a certain level of creativity; some just have more than others. How does creativity manifest itself in the workplace? What's the best work environment for creativity? What products (tangible or otherwise) are creative? Where does that creativity arise from? And what acts, behaviors etc, may be examples of the organizational creative process? What risks are associated with creativity not being manifested in the workplace? How might you see creativity in employees?

- **Creativity is a "domain" contextualized competency:** Let's face it, most businesses are interested in visible results; then first needed is a tool to assess how creative the business (or employee, department or product etc.) is. Next, specific strategies can be put in place to target the areas identified as "lacking" in creativity. Finally, a tool could be used again to "measure" improvements. Coping strategies for the mundane, painful, stressful, tiring, challenging or competitive nature of many working environments requires developing often elaborate routines in order to weave some form of personal creative narrative through their day-to-day existence. People have to be given the opportunity to be creative, they have to become empowered. Business leaders should be aware that a quantitative measure would not be a perfect solution, but the importance of creativity for organizations is well-known, yet there is no adequate way of assessing the concept in the workplace. Creativity in the workplace is fundamentally about the mental production of new ideas - not just any new ideas, but the creation of ideas that are both original and valuable. Everyone has the ability to create, but creativity is an inherent ability that cannot be taught, only developed. In fact, those who aren't creative find it almost alien to be creative. Possessing the ability of creative foresight is not a skill that everyone possesses. Developing a creative workplace requires the deliberate creation of original and valuable ideas when they are needed - they need to be created on-demand.

- **The innovators are likely to make a change to the structure for better problem solving:** The way we manage structure (the paradox of structure, actually) has a marked impact on how we deal with problems and the types of solutions we envisage. The workplace needs to be designed to help employees at all levels within an organization (from leaders to front-line) understand and develop their creative capacity to solve problems and exploit opportunities in new and innovative ways. The tool utilizes cutting-edge narrow band psychometrics to diagnose, assess and train the core factors of creativity such as, cognitive processes, personality, motivation, and capacity. The more innovative the employees are, the less tolerant of structure (policies, rules and paradigms) and less respectful of consensus they are. Innovators often prefer to "do things differently" and such major re-molding or breaking of paradigms means loosening structure and challenging consensus until the new way is adopted and becomes the new structure or paradigm. Innovators are likely to make a change to the current structure (from within which the problem emerged) in order to solve it. They then make further changes as an outcome of using the solution.

- **There are two types of measurement of creativity**: The problem for building a creative workplace is being able to create a measure that assesses the different dimensions of organizational creativity adequately while keeping it general enough to assess this in a wide range of organizations and job roles. Generally speaking, there are two types of measurement: The first type of measurement of creativity in the workplace is through the results, the outcomes of creative thoughts and actions. What value have those new things designed and implemented (products, services, processes, business models) brought to customers or users? There are various metrics for this - the number of patents, new products, R&D spending, etc. The second type of assessment is through the innovation drivers, the elements that enhance an organization's innovation capacity. For measuring such, there must be an appreciation for the organization of the sources of creativity as well as the structures and cultures that will promote innovation. Talent, the individual, and teamwork are important, so are strategy, system and processes, so are the freedom and a capacity for risk-taking. Innovation management in the workplace is a multi-dimensional pursuit.

Even without formal assessment, one can see that in creative organizations, people are encouraged and given the time and resources to work on new things that excite them, all are required to produce new ideas, people are often trained in creative methods and techniques, the business model is often challenged, everyone has a personal creativity objective at work and there is much humor to go around.

4 Three Practices of Digital Innovation

Either at the individual or organizational level, creativity is the critical success factor to achieve the digital vision.

Generally speaking, innovation is to transform novel ideas to achieve their business values. It is not serendipity, but a discipline and a set of practices to achieve business goals. Innovation helps to tackle the complexities of business dynamic in the digital ecosystem, but often within itself, it needs to change and improve as well. Therefore, digital paradigm shift also includes the perspective of building a scalable innovation environment or innovation ecosystem. It is crucial to fine-tune innovation processes, capabilities, and develop a set of practices to manage innovation portfolio more effectively.

- **Systematic Innovation**: Innovation can be viewed as consisting of many different stages such as, idea generation, development, and implementation. Creativity stage is generally accepted to be less structured than development stage, and the later is likely to be far more process driven than the former. A systematic innovation approach is to depict innovation as a system rather than a traditional process; its performance depends on the alignment of various business components such as people, resources, information & technologies, actions, control, etc. Thus, systematic innovation practice means to manage innovation, not as a one-time initiative, but a structured way with fine-tuned processes and a set of practical tools used to create or improve product/service/process that delivers value-added solutions to delight customers or engage employees. Even for the "soft flavored innovations," such as communication, management, or culture innovation, it is important to have some degree of a "hard-wired" innovation system to translate into business processes or change mechanisms with the proper metrics to monitor it. Though such structures or processes shouldn't be overly rigid to stifle innovation. The systematic innovation is based on the in-depth understanding of business issues, it's important to do the systematic analysis of the true business problems, opportunities, or dilemmas, and then, the practice of systematic innovation can focus on mapping and aligning the important business elements to solve them in a structured way.

- **Intrapreneurship or corporate
  entrepreneurship:** Compared to nimble startups,
  many well-established organizations are struggling
  with innovation, due to the legacy technologies or
  processes, silo thinking, change inertia, or overly
  rigid hierarchy. So,what are the strategies or
  practices to advocate innovation in those
  companies? Intrapreneurship is considered as a
  relatively recent concept to practice innovation in
  large organizations to close innovation gaps,
  especially for business model innovation, it runs up
  against a "not now, later" obstacle. For example, if
  a well-established organization identifies a new
  value proposition that requires the change on the
  business model or creates the new one, and then,
  it's strategically safer to develop the new venture
  and run it with faster speed. Now many
  organizations that are in the digital journey also run
  in bimodal speed, to strike the right balance
  between stability and innovation, efficiency and
  agility. Overall speaking, corporate
  entrepreneurship is embodying risk-taking and more
  radical changes, but it helps the company to develop
  either the new business or the unique capability to
  create revenue and improve the top line growth,
  promote and sustain organizational performance

and renew the business energy to be a digital disruptor, rather than "being disrupted."

- **Hybrid Innovation:** We live in the business world with physical corporate buildings and remote working environment, the hybrid of many things from energy to technologies, etc. It is hard to think of any innovation without a hybrid nature, a combination of something old with something new, or a number of new things. And digitalization is mainly an incremental-radical innovation continuum. Often the potential benefits from innovation and risks are proportional. The incremental innovation starts with small objectives, aims to achieve business improvement (products/service/process), and brings short-term value additions; while radical innovation often starts with a problem or a challenge, having no solution in the current situation, it may have "creatively disruptive" characteristics, it brings something new, something that couldn't have been possible without innovation, and it shows amazingly differentiated business value for the long term, but it could mean to take the certain level of risks. Therefore, innovation portfolio management does require keeping the hybrid theme and leveraging the variety of business factors, not just having the interdisciplinary understanding of connecting the dots and seeing what's possible, but also having the technical expertise to create the multifaceted values, and even disruptions if necessary.

Either at the individual or organizational level, creativity and innovation become one of the most critical success factors to achieve the digital vision. It is the core activity of digital evolution. The speed of innovation also needs to be accelerated, so that the flow of innovation will have reached a new level, a level that can address the "VUCA" challenges of digital dynamic.

5 How to Fine Tune the Organizational Structure for Breakthrough Innovation

An organizational structure carries inherent capabilities as to what can be achieved within its frame.

Innovation is to transform novel ideas and achieve their business value. However, for most organizations, innovation, especially breakthrough innovation, is still serendipitous. There are many factors to decide innovation success. From an organizational structure perspective, how can you get well organized for managing innovation more effectively?

- **The right structure is the one that allows the right mentality and culture to bloom:** There are both official structure and unofficial structure in the organization. If there is a strong mentality of invention and innovation, will a rigid official structure be just ignored in favor of an unofficial structure? Or shall you strive for an aligned official structure to enable innovation, rather than relying on people establishing unofficial structures? The structure carries inherent capabilities as to what can be achieved within its frame. A misaligned structure can reinforce a non-innovation friendly climate, and though a strong mentality may be able to overcome it, it will certainly require both dedication and effort. Within a well-aligned structure, that dedication and effort may be spent on innovation efforts rather than overcoming organizational hurdles and pushing against structural boundaries.

- **The official structure and unofficial structure can co-exist harmoniously**: It's no surprise that unofficial structures always exist. The question is only whether the official structure and the unofficial structure co-exist antagonistically or harmoniously. A poorly designed official structure can increase the likelihood of antagonism between the two. An unofficial structure may always exist to some degree, and for good reasons, but would not go as far as to say that the question is only about alignment, because it would imply that a strong unofficial structure is as desirable as a strong official one. So given the opportunity, establishing a formal and enabling structure in line with your ambition and desired direction, and nurturing a culture within it, is preferable to relying on individuals and groups to overcome the hurdles of existing within a structure that inherently is not designed for the innovation.

- **The different organizational models have different inherent capabilities:** They are as such ease efforts towards certain directions, respective to each model. There is a limit to what an unofficial structure can structurally accomplish. The challenge is that an unofficial structure may spread cynicism in the organization. At the same time, it may be a strong ally in innovation and change. It is necessary to identify the unofficial structures and take them along on the journey of innovation and change. Also, establishing some of the more advanced models will certainly require top management awareness, involvement, dedication, and can by no means be unofficial. Because different models carry different capabilities, the choice of model will impact your ability to execute on your defined innovation strategy and direct efforts towards strategically prioritized targets.

- **Ideally, the unofficial structure that has emerged over time is the formal structure you should have:** Change can only happen in a context that takes heed of current culture and unwritten rules; identifying how to change is very much about identifying where you are now. After all, where you presently stand determines the path you have to take to get to where you want to be. As such, present official and unofficial structures are certainly part of a change journey. Organizations should incorporate and leverage what official and unofficial structures one might have into the journey's end-state, but only as long as they are used to where you want to go. Ideally, the unofficial structure that has emerged over time is the formal structure you should have. But, not all unofficial structures are helpful in this sense, in that they have been formed in response to an incumbent formal structure and strategic context, so they carry the legacy and lack relevance within a new formal structure and context. Going forward, it may well require changing both official and unofficial structures into a hybrid structure that can support an innovation journey in the direction you are heading, rather than where you have been.

- **A lightweight process allows innovation to turn into value:** Innovation is undirected and ineffective without some kind of structure. Innovation is based on creativity. Creativity is subversive because it challenges the status quo. Rules are about safeguarding the status quo. Consequently, too rigid rules will stifle creativity and thus innovation. Innovation challenges the status quo and that is important in a healthy, innovative organization. An organization that has a lightweight process which allows creativity and innovation to flow, get protected, channeled and nurtured will succeed more often than an organization that does not have such a process.

- **You need to change the mentality. And that is not easy:** What needs to worry is the danger of a company adopting a couple of simple rules without doing the difficult work to change the mentality. Because such an approach won't have any favorable effect. It might even have an adverse effect on feeding cynicism in the company. Resistance to change is then often camouflaged by talking about the experience. The organization has to be open to innovation and rules can't change that. Rules alone will not allow innovation to be productive. A framework is needed for innovation to be successful. Part of putting a framework in place is getting senior leaders to recognize that innovation is important and needs to be supported. Senior leadership support (or, at least, a change champion) is required for innovation to be successful (create value for the organization). This has to include the tolerance of failure, because innovation is a learning process, and in learning failures occur. These failures are tolerable and even valuable if people learn from them and use what they learned in their next project.

It is really hard to be a consistently innovative company, it requires fine-tuning the organizational structure and culture (the collective mindset) that nurtures new ideas and is able to profitably execute on those ideas. This is not easy, and companies that strive for innovation must experiment and learn to organize for both breakthrough innovation and continuous improvement and build innovation capability cohesively.

6 Innovating the Digital-Ready Boardroom

Modern board directors are innovators who can break down the old rules, and set digital principles to inspire businesses stepping into the new chapter of digital innovation.

The corporate board plays a crucial role in providing strategy oversights and makes sound judgments and assurance of corporate actions within a framework of practical knowledge. Innovation is one of the most important ingredients in the business strategy, which role should BoDs play in both management innovation and innovation management? And how to develop the best and next practices for innovating the boardroom?

- **Innovation is absolutely a mindset:** Boards as top leadership teams should participate or even lead in the area of both innovation management and management innovation. Although the major responsibility of Boards is for practicing governance, it doesn't mean to stifle innovation; on the opposite, it means to set principles and build the right framework for managing innovation in an effective way. An innovative board brings the outliers' fresh eyes, out-of-the-box thinking or bigger box thinking capability, and a tremendous set of skills and experience mix to create new value, and contribute to both innovation management and innovation governance.

- **Innovation should be embedded in every aspect of the organization, including strategy:**
Innovation is what leads to differentiation. There are many ways to differentiate, and therefore, there are many ways to build innovation into a corporate strategy. Boards oversee strategies, and therefore, boards need to pay more attention to innovation. A good strategy will include where the company plans to focus its innovation efforts such as product performance, cost-effectiveness, speed, business model, etc, how this links to the rest of the corporate goals, and action plan must be put in place to achieve the innovation goals. The board should ask how the enterprise measures innovation and how it compares to "Best in Class" performance and be sure the measurement is accurate from the eyes of the customers and their constituencies. One important role the Board must play in making sure management reports on whether and how

investments in innovation are yielding forecast results. Whether it is about managing a major IT project, launching a product, or reshaping culture, assuring excellence in predicting and tracking results falls in the domain of anyone with fiduciary responsibility.

- **Innovation needs the certain level of guidelines and rules:** Digital brings both unprecedented opportunities and risks to the businesses today. Every innovation pursuit has risks in it, and every risk has opportunities in it. Therefore, it is important to set guidelines for managing innovation risks in a structural way. BoDs can make the proper policies to encourage innovation and manage risks. It requires acknowledgment, involvement, and commitment. The principles and guidelines help to further frame processes, practices, measures, and control.

Innovation is too important to leave solely in the hands of the management team without any oversight or guidance. Innovation governance needs to advocate, steer, and sustain innovation. Thus digital directorship today must be extremely visionary, mindful, creative, empathetic, generous, conscious, passionate, and humble. Modern board directors are also innovators themselves who can break the old rules, and build digital principles to inspire businesses stepping into the next chapter of digital innovation blossoms.

7 Embedding Creativity in Change Management

The change shall not always be stressful and reactive; make it as fun and proactive as possible.

Too often changes are made as a reaction to outer impulses, crisis, and demands. This is the bureaucratic way of meeting the challenges. The perspective is often rational, an automatic cultural response; defending already existing structures, all that we take for granted, without questioning the underlying premises. In order to make change both proactive and sustainable, how to embed creative mechanism in change management?

- **At the enterprise level, successful change is often linked to the DNA of the organization itself**: Change needs to be embedded into the business culture, it's particularly important for those creative industries or organizations that have extensive innovative product development regimes. It would follow that the use of creativity would be more welcome in these areas, than perhaps industries where it is not openly valued, a heavily regulated or controlled business, but regardless of vertical sector, make change a fun and innovative journey, not just a stressful one-time project.

- **Exploring ways to satisfy key players takes a lot of creativity:** Each company has a different agenda and rarely is it centered on what's best for the organization. Creativity is a key to satisfying these agendas and achieving the benefits of the change. It's what keeps things moving forward and actually gets the programs delivered. The main perspective or focus is usually either outside in or inside out. The outside-in is too often the approach for change management; we try to make a difference by shaking the old bottle, stirring up the existing structures and patterns, without shifting either the bottle or the content. Or we try to condition to the circumstances, still dancing with the same partner; in a context where the answer is to change the fundamental premises with creativity.

- **Creativity today asks for a new mindset:** Real change and (existential) creativity is deprogramming old mindsets, letting go of "the voices from the past," reprogramming our minds with new values, norms, and attitudes; establishing a new blueprint for how we want to create our future reality. This is a task for visionary or entrepreneur-minded leaders to convey and make an impact, as traditional management may not agile enough to adapt to the changes. Creativity is incredibly useful, both in terms of making an impact with change management communications and tactics. Because these days, it is pretty tough to get attention as there is so much going on, but also in terms of strategies and solutions. Still we need all approaches to succeed for the overall betterment.

- **At the project/small group levels, there is no reason why creativity cannot or does not form part of the Change Management practices:** From the workshops through to implementation, it is CREATION that always questioning everything, not only that seems proper to the management, pleasing existing patterns and positions. To succeed, businesses need a united "one sight" focus, a dynamic balance between the inner and outer, "yin" and "yang," dancing together. We need to deeply understand the relation and dynamics between consciousness (thinking), energy (emotions) and information, the manifested creativity is so important to change management; it can serve as a tool for cognitive dissonance to support adoption. When developing a change strategy, think of a creative mechanism that has this outcome to embed the change.

- **At the individual level, human beings are not only 'reasonable' but they have imagination**: Change is good and we must embrace and adapt to it. All happens through imagination and change is living. There cannot be any change without imagination, which means creativity; being creative helps in discovering new solutions, in working differently and building a new world. Overall speaking, to overcome resistance, we need to feel safe, to overcome our fear, to be convinced that the new solutions are better than the old ones.

We need to be so deeply motivated and invigorated that we realize and stick to the three most evaluated qualities of life: **AUTONOMY, MASTERY, and MEANING**. This can only be effectuated by empathy and wisdom, Reduce the fear of real change, and we give way to a new, playful creativity. Indeed, change is a strategic imperative; make it a creative journey, not a stressful project.

8 How to Base your New Innovations on Known Customer Needs?

Digital is the age of customer empathy.

Innovation is about how to transform novel ideas and achieve its commercial values. Customers should be the center of innovation management and they are the major focus for innovation process and accomplishment. For most of the organizations, innovation is still the serendipity, but being customer-centric is the ultimate goals of those organizations, how should you base your new product innovation on known customer needs?

- **Focusing on customers' needs should be an easier path to grow innovation fruits:** Shaping "customer desire" is a different task from shaping or understanding "need"; and making consumers believe their "want" is a "need" is a recipe for success. If you're going to innovate without knowledge of "evident customer needs," and then, the things that you are good at may distract you to build something which can really increase customer value and help business success for the long term. Always train to take a step back, put yourself in the customer's shoes and think as they would like to have. First, understand customers' needs, and then, you can look at the company's technical capabilities. Innovation should come in the common area of technical competence, customer needs, and profitability. You might produce the most-sophisticated-in- the market product, but no one needs and buys it, that will waste talent and resource of business. It will be easier to develop an innovative product in order to satisfy a need or shortcoming; rather than manipulating the whole environment and market so that you can define what the customer should need.

- **How to frame the right questions to get the best feedback from customers:** It's tricky to find the right mix of open-ended questions to get the feedback you wouldn't have thought about and more precise questions to actually get the customer to think of something he/she wouldn't have thought about. Shall you ask broader questions or shall you initiate more narrow questions, every company just has to take a good look at which information would be the most valuable to them and tailor their questions accordingly. It is important to capture customer insight, not just getting information and understand it partially. The value of customer feedback is in transforming it from information to insight and using this to interpret customer needs. Sometimes we forget that customers are not that great at answering certain types of questions accurately, they don't exactly know what they want until they see it, but they know what they dislike, or they can well articulate which features they expect from their perspective. Hence, it doesn't mean you shouldn't ask, just how you should interpret the results, and capture the insight based on the information you get carefully.

- **The mechanics of gamification works to facilitate customer interaction and collaboration seamlessly:** When you are engaged with customers and invite them to co-think and co-create the outcome depends on what, how and who is asked. A lot of companies claim they want to engage their customers, to make them more satisfied and increase interactions, but the hard part is getting everyone on board and have a methodology to do that. The gamification mechanics helps engage customers in more fun, but perhaps more effective way. Because it gives people a measurable way to earn the respect of their peers.

Customers can be very useful in providing feedback about future new products/services, helping improve current processes. But the true innovation in the product comes from allowing people free reign to try ideas, it requires a culture of cooperation and collaboration, of constant pushing of the boundaries as proposed in the discipline of innovation leaders. Innovation is a symphony which needs to be orchestrated via seamless synchronization and effortless collaboration.

Chapter 6

Innovation Paradox

The purpose of Innovation Management is not to promote innovation, but to manage innovation as a process.

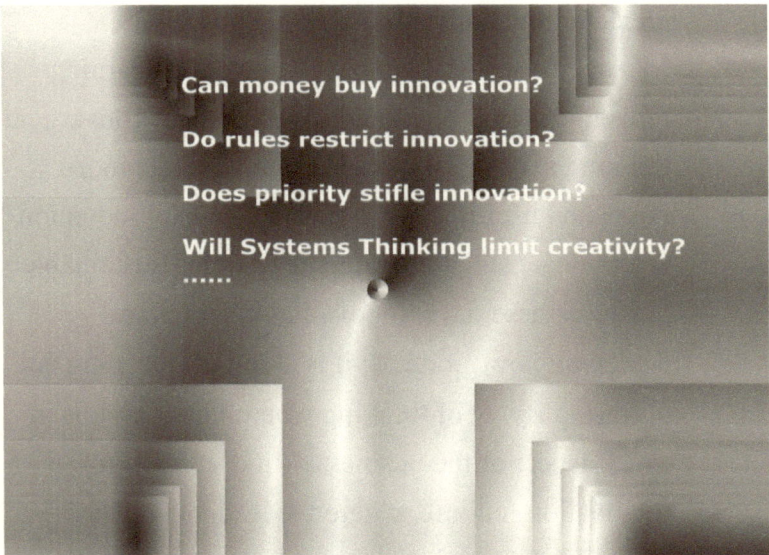

Figure 10 Innovation Paradox

Innovation is to transform the novel ideas and achieve their business value. Innovation is not just about generating ideas or exchanging ideas, based on most of the innovation models; idea creation is only one step of the innovation process. Therefore, in a basic view, innovation is a process and every process needs to be managed. But what's the best approach to managing innovation? There is the deduced question: Is innovation management a waste? Can you transform an idea into sustainable benefit without Innovation Management?

- **Innovativeness is absolutely a mindset:** You will create/enforce this mindset via Innovation Management (IM)! People can leverage learning tools to develop both their divergent and convergent thinking skills. They can learn to generate more novel and useful ideas in diverse teams. Innovation is a mindset and a prerequisite to doing sustainable business these days. Innovation is more than designing new products; it is about establishing and nurturing a way of thinking where innovation is in every aspect of the business. Mindset leads to (innovation) culture, where the leadership has to understand that it is the process. As an organization, you need to manage your strategic directions, your process, capabilities of your people to create a much more innovative organization.

- **Innovation Culture (IC) is like Safety Culture:** You have to live it and breathe it every day, otherwise, you get injured. In the case of IM, you are really talking about how to manage resources (people, assets) to meet a new innovation objective. They are two very different things. IC is a mindset, a way of doing things, risk-taking, doing things differently, asking hard questions, failing and being able to fail again without repercussions. It is the organizational culture that you need as the grassroots of innovation. Management has to align its objectives with its culture, otherwise, it is a lip service and no true innovation can occur. Also, innovation can occur anywhere in the organization, and frankly, it has to occur in every aspect of the organization. People have to question why things are done in a certain way, why people use products in a certain way, what products the customer doesn't even know they want, why certain processes are done in certain ways, etc. Innovation cultures are behaviors towards innovation within the organization. Cultures are the patterns of behavior towards something: What is the organization's innovation culture? Behavior towards innovation within the organization. At the 1st place, to what extent the innovation is actively embraced by every group of employees, whether C-levels allow and foster innovation processes. In that respect, innovation "policies, programs and structures" are the result of IC. If IC is poor, innovation tools will not be in place and vice versa. Organizations really need some kind of "spark" to initiate the seed of IC. The things are often missing in advocating are the consequences of poor innovation culture. So, primarily you have to change the culture, then come "policies, programs, and structures "! And to change IC, you have to primarily change top leadership. How you intend to change policies that govern the innovation process, if C-levels are against? They will not allow the internals changing anything and they will not hire external innovators! If you are not planning to apply policies, programs and structures to change the culture, and then what are you planning to use? These are the three tools that management has to create the desired culture.

- **IM needs to take a balanced approach**: It is invaluable in the management of the innovation workflow, decision-making, and development process framework. IM is a way to manage the spend for R&D, just like stage gate and other project management and decision tools. IM is a set of tools for managers to oversee and report on product/process/idea development. IM needs to establish the framework to manage innovation in a systematic way. People can learn several things relating to creativity and these can come under the heading of innovation management. For example, people can learn a process to define the innovation challenge, generate and select ideas, plan for these to be implemented. They can do this so that better ideas get tested quicker and learned about faster. No doubt about it. Second, people can learn about their own problem-solving style. However, overly rigid IM processes discourage innovation, because such management is about bureaucracy and innovation is about creativity. But if we say that IM is opposite to innovation and IM kills innovation, then it is the extreme which makes more harm than benefit! Take a balanced approach; provide maximal freedom for ideators, then straightforward process for converting an idea into an innovation. Maybe special attention has to be focused on idea assessment part of the IM process. If the process requests from ideators to elaborate on the 20-pages form of their idea, ending with SWOTs, feasibility studies, and business cases, then it is lousy IM process design! It is also impossible to make innovation at risk level reaching zero! And effectively, when IM is oriented like that, the only thing possible is to move backward. In fact, IM has to bring strategy to allow ideation and creativity growing unencumbered, and to pick up the ideas that will become innovation.

- **There are three factors need to line up for innovation to flourish:** Innovation Management is a process tool which per se neither drives innovation competence nor innovation results. It is one of the three factors which need to line up for innovation to flourish. The other two are the existence of an explicit innovation strategy and a company culture which fosters innovation. All three factors need to have long-term top management commitment and personal support. Delegation does not work here. Innovation management is not about generating innovative ideas, but rather the processes to take ideas to value. In this process, certain ideas or opportunities will have more business appeal than others - and given that resources are limited. The IM process 'should' enable focus on most attractive opportunities. If a company's IM process is charged with 'creating the ideas,' it will likely become ineffective and stifle to the innovation mindset. If IM also provides a mechanism for the organization to freely express ideas and for these to be built upon, and then this model can greatly enhance idea generation within the business.

- **It's critical to strike the right balance between ideation and execution part of the innovation process:** Far too many innovation management experts excel in helping their organizations create ideas but come short in the other two phases of innovation. Before ideation, companies need to discover insights. After ideation, companies need to filter, prototype and validate their ideas. Far from stifling the production of ideas, managed ideation produces far more ideas than unmanaged brainstorming and thinking do. The quality of those ideas, however, depends on the insights that fuel them. The results of those ideas depend on the ability of the company to select the best ones, develop them and implement them. The true root of the challenge stems from either knowing or not knowing what you want to be to whom! Companies or brands that understand and execute against that filter daily are far more likely to be successful in the long run.

- **It's a matter of measurement:** The problem is that the KPIs to measure success in business have so often been predominantly financial in nature. The leading indicators for successful innovation are not financial, and most Innovation Management initiatives are not successful and are incredibly wasteful. The key is to properly measure their success behaviors and hold them accountable. There is the standard way of measuring the innovation performance in the company such as share of profit or revenue generated from innovation. Of course, it is not easy to define how much was generated from innovation, but there are rough estimates of new products, improved products, and cost savings due to innovation in internal processes.

If you don't have IM process in place, it is substantially harder and less likely to be an innovative company for the long run. It means that your processes will be less safe and economic and products are more expensive or with lower quality. Creativity results in ideas but until those ideas are actualized they will remain ideas. It is only after the ideas are implemented, then they become innovations. That is innovation management.

1 Can Money Buy Innovation

The business innovation success is not always proportional to how much money you pour in.

It is very important to recognize that innovation is an essential factor for the business success. Organizations need both: Out of the box and in the box/core innovation; both breakthrough innovation and incremental and evolutionary innovation, but how to accomplish this balance is a crucial issue for organizations. From innovation management perspective, what're the resources and key success factors to lead innovation success, can money buy innovation?

- **The business innovation success is not always proportional to how much money you pour in:** There is an underlying assumption that ideation can be done if you invest more. However, based on the variety of innovation studies, the business innovation success is not always proportional to how much money you invest in. Meaningful new products are available simply by applying the effort of creative people. So, consider this logic:
(a) If this were the case and if money could accelerate the effort applied;
(b) if companies were willing to reward new product innovation;
(c) if new products / Blue Ocean strategies are far more valuable than Red Ocean/ sustaining strategies and so incentivize companies to pursue, wouldn't we be flooded with new products and then the leading companies would be flooded with profits? If this is true and is so apparently obvious, wouldn't we see more examples of it happening in the business world?

- **Money facilitates innovation, but not guarantees the result**: As the variety of research shows that money does improve some outcomes of the innovation process. What you are primarily doing is harvesting ideas that have emerged and are waiting to be picked. The money will increase the willingness of employees to give you those ideas. It doesn't mean though that it will increase the volume of ideas that are available to be collected. The research also shows that money does improve some outcomes of the innovation process - as does a plethora of non-monetary rewards. There are many human links within the innovation phases and usually implemented in teams. What inspires and motivates many innovators is the passion for learning new things with a focus on new technologies and for understanding how they work. They want to make a difference in learning and development, to do meaningful work and to develop new applications and products that can help other people learn faster and better and do great things. Money is important, but it's not the only thing matters.

- **Reward risk-taking to build a culture of innovation**: The failures should not be rewarded, but they should be understood and not penalized. And surely risk-taking also should be supported - morally at least. Does incentivizing alone solve all the problems? Of course not. This is an important finding given a popular assertion that incentivizing innovation with money doesn't work at all. It's about a "culture of innovation" which incorporates multiple and diverse components. It doesn't mean you should reward "failure" as such; but to inspire the culture of innovation, you should rather reward taking risks. The culture of innovation starts with a culture of participation because employee engagement in the innovation process increases participation. Innovation does not have a chance without top management support and commitment. The first step to drive innovation within an organization is to commit to it and develop the capability to innovate, from discovery (front-end) to development (middle) then deployment (back-end). It's about setting a cultural adjustment and understanding within the organization that innovation is embraced and expected, including the acceptance of failure along the path to innovation and ensuring the culture supports that versus penalizing innovation that doesn't initially (or ever) work out. Staff won't embrace innovation in a bold manner if failures associated with it hamper their career growth or tarnish their reputation within the organization.

It seems that many companies going through a period of introspection believe that they already implicitly understand the nature of innovation. All too often they perhaps manage a few innovation projects successfully, but they lack the systematic approach to manage resources, to bridge talent gaps, to build a culture of innovation and to shape the business level of innovation capability. There are multiple factors beyond money in innovation success, which will bring multi-dimensional values to drive business success.

2 Do Rules Restrict innovation

**Breaking rules is indeed an important part of creativity.
Innovation needs a level of guidance.**

Innovation is to transform novel ideas and achieve their
business value. It is a business discipline which can be
managed. In many organizations, perhaps there is an
innovation department specifically setting the rules to take
charge of innovation. The paradox is that all creative
activities are subversive in questioning the status quo.
Setting rules and goals for creativity goes against the very
nature of creativity and thus inventiveness and innovation.
So does innovation department stifle innovation? Isn't there
a more fundamental problem with innovation failures?
What should be done if the rest of the company is hostile to
innovation? Should the company give up on innovation?

- **Breaking rules is indeed an important part of
  creativity**: Ideas should never be evaluated
  (referring to criteria and goals) in the ideation
  phase. However, 'business creativity' such as using
  creative thinking for business goals, does require
  certain 'rules.' To get the best results, you need to
  structure the creative process. For instance,

depending on where you are in the process, you might want to 'force' people to rephrase a challenge, let them view an idea from different perspectives, temporarily forbid criticism, set time limits, apply thinking techniques, each with their own 'rules' etc. It seems that the more integrated and culturally based innovation or imagination is, the more sustainable and productive such initiatives are. If an innovation department operates without being an integral part of every other department, it certainly could be counterproductive. Therefore, overly rigid process or too 'pushy' goals will stifle inventiveness and innovation.

- **Innovation needs a level of guidance:** Innovation has to deliver business objectives; otherwise, it is just an invention. The innovation leader needs to become a master at persuasive communications through proposals, pitches, scenarios, analysis and stories that might resonate with the company. You can only do as much as you are "invested" in the company. It's complicated. The truth is that companies will succeed if they have the right chemistry and others will fail because they don't. If the truth is considered "destructive negativism" that culture must change or it eventually will self-destruct. Innovation is somewhere between invention and implementation - finding new and different ways of doing things. Innovation is doing something better than it currently is. Hence, it requires a sound and competent understanding of what is currently being done. Not what others are good at. It's a mindset.

- **Innovation Management needs the right kind of governance to thrive:** Practically speaking, when there is an innovative idea; the governance mechanisms dictate how that idea is fostered from inception to retirement. Traditional business governance for an operational excellence enterprise will discourage innovation. If innovation management is like the pedal to accelerate the speed of the car, and then business governance is the steering wheel to keep a straight line or take a turn at that velocity of strategic planning processes and business execution scenario; the headlights to do forecasting of what lays ahead (risk or opportunity); fuel gauge, speedometer to measure; the brakes to slow or continue (resource management) etc. Governance needs to set the framework for innovation management as an enabling approach. Governance by definition does not set corporate strategy that is management's responsibility. Governance does not define company culture, which is one of the key contributors/enablers for innovation. Remember governance isn't just about putting restrictions on what you can do, it is also about monitoring and knowing when things are not going to plan so that you can take appropriate actions at the right time.

- **Never give up, or you risk obsolescence:**
Spreading awareness about market trends in your industry and with your competitors can aid motivation. It's also helpful to perform whatever type of analysis/research that's possible to ask several "levels of why" to learn more about the roots of the resistance to innovation. All you need is a handful of courageous change agents to move an entire company forward. The most difficult situation is when a company has been successful in the past, and people do not want to accept that the old business model is sinking. In industries looking decline in the eyes, the same phenomenon can be observed. People don't believe that their company is in danger of perishing because they just cannot or don't want to see it. Any differing view is

considered destructive negativism. Dealing with such a situation is quite a challenge.

The business is complex, the people are complex, and the world is complex. It takes out-of-the-box thinking and open leadership style to spark innovation. But the right set of rule and governance framework are also important for innovation enablement and complexity management under today's "VUCA" working dynamic in order to achieve business value from innovation.

3 Does Prioritization Stifle Creativity?

Prioritization needs to provide a framework for focusing on creativity.

A company has finite resources to apply to get the best yield possible to meet a stakeholder expectation. So there're always some constraints for businesses to explore the new opportunities or deploy the new ideas, therefore, evaluation and prioritization are taken place to leverage resources in project or innovation management. Does it mean such prioritization process will stifle creativity?

- **Evaluation vs. prioritization**: Creativity can be in the form of an idea, a solution, an approach, etc. It is up to the idea proposer to show it is worthwhile. Evaluation is where creativity lives or dies -

depending on the nature, culture and needs of the organization. Evaluation should ask, "Is this a good idea?" and "Can we do it?" Prioritization then asks, "Is this the best use of our resources, now?" Prioritization is about managing constraints - you can't do everything; so which projects will you do? The key is to separate 'Evaluation' of ideas from "Prioritization."

- **Prioritization enables strategic focus**: Prioritization brings transparency to the organization, creating internal competition among new ideas and projects. Prioritization forces people to be more creative, to come up with better ideas, because now they know that their ideas will be discussed at the board level, and if chosen, they will be followed closely. In addition, prioritization helps to focus the strategy of the organization, which has huge benefits in terms of execution.

- **In general, prioritization increases creativity and does not decrease it**: But the term has a different semantic connotation, and each situation is different, so there is always going to be lots of different opinions. If you prioritize across all projects, you know which projects should get that extra increment of analysis and design effort. Creativity typically comes from having some slack resources that you can apply to problem-solving.

- **The risk-averse corporate culture could also be the issue to stifle creativity:** Some organizations are open to new ideas and others resistant, it doesn't depend on whether there is a prioritization process or not. Corporations do need to prioritize. They also need a process by which evaluation of those priorities occurs and through that process review new ideas, revisions or changes, and just the killing floor of non-productive projects, programs, or activities on the prioritized list.

- **An overly complex process can easily stifle innovation:** Sometimes innovations fail when organizations get locked into huge processes around building extensive business cases. You may also refer to cases where the prioritization process is not well implemented, not respected, people use tricks to cheat the system, or eventually when the process becomes more important than the content and the goal, or too bureaucratic, which is when creativity is stifled. In all these cases, the issue is not prioritization.

- **Prioritization provides a framework for focusing on the creativity**: It's only if the actual work is micromanaged and regulated to the point where resources are not able to create, and then creativity becomes stifled. Prioritization is also the process and method that one communicates either top down or bottom up and impacts how a creative approach, idea, or project is received in an organization. If you have two somewhat conflicting needs - high quality and low cost for example, you can apply creative techniques to achieve both. Prioritization of requirements can be an excellent augmentation to creativity in this case.

- **Prioritization is critical – as the alternative is a land grab for resources**: It is usually suboptimal and damaging, especially when legitimate top priorities are delayed while pet projects are fully staffed. Since the projects have different investment considerations - for example, risk reduction for maintenance work, ROI for tactical and some strategic work, and organization learning measures for true innovation work. So the objective shouldn't be to work on only those projects for which you have staff, it should be to maximize what you can accomplish through creative leverage of your talent pool.

Thereof, good process design should encourage creativity by giving people space to be creative and including evaluation of creativity as part of that process. If companies don't make room in the prioritization process for projects that have significant risks but also potentially significant upside results, it can, in fact, drive creative thinkers out of an organization. "Creativity" and "progress" don't always mean greater risks, but often the two go hand-in-hand if you are looking for breakthroughs or real innovation.

4 Does Systems Thinking Limit Creativity or not?

Creativity is an outcome of a deep understanding of the patterns thinking that underlies Systems Thinking.

Creativity is an inward process to produce the novel ideas and build unique value. Creativity is by definition an aspect of the emergent behavior that exists within us and the emergent traits that extend from us to the surrounding world. Creativity is infused with an inner cohesion and comes from a vision of uniqueness. Systems thinking is the thought process to understand the interconnectivity between parts and the whole. But does Systems Thinking stifle creativity or not?

- **Systems Thinking wouldn't stifle creativity:** We humans tend to be very fixed in our definitions and Systems Thinking is a great candidate for such boundary - yet in practice doesn't mean restricting anything. In fact, when used properly, it can enhance creativity to a great extent and push it to very high levels. It surely provides the direction to think creatively. For example, simply by observing self-organizing patterns of complex systems, one may get deep creative ideas about the most appropriate actions to be taken. Thinking systemically actually helps the resulting creativity and innovation by forcing yet more ingenuity, rigor, and precision into the approach.

- **Leveraging Systems thinking in harnessing innovation is all about taking a scientific approach for problem identifying and solving**: It allows you to a number of things: Embrace uncertainty, identify interconnections and interdependencies, understand flows or the lack of them, and identify business opportunities. Once you have a comprehensive vision of the system and its characteristics and dynamics, creativity is essential in order to propose changes, improvements, disruptions, etc. Creative thinking, Systems Thinking, and many other thought processes are all interlinked attributes we bring to our respective crafts in varying degrees depending on our mental models, perspectives, distinctions, etc, but how this manifest itself in each of us is unique, and then such interlinks often fuels new thoughts, perspectives, creativity and the imagination to spark into the fountain of new ideas and keep creativity flow.

- **Creativity is an outcome of a deep understanding of the patterns thinking that underlies Systems Thinking:** There are "common structures" that can be used for the purpose of creativity that is produced by combining different patterns of Systems Thinking. A systems thinker without creativity ends up as a caretaker or administrator. A creative person without systemic thinking might lack structure frame to keep focus. Systems thinking, and thinking, in general, is more about discovery than about creativity, invention, and originality. Creativity to some extent is the nature of seeing the patterns that already exist, and then being able to predict how they change, and sometimes manipulate them in a direction that fits our needs or that of our objective.

- **Systems Thinking keeps in mind a global or macro perspective:** The true System Thinking is about seeing the connections around us. The only way Systems Thinking would inhibit creativity is if the fullest global perspective is not kept in one's mind's eye when evaluating the sub-systems. If creativity is about solving problems in new and unusual ways, might systems thinking, inadvertently stifle creativity if it did not embrace the potential benefits of contribution from differential culture and class. Say, there is a marvelous system of creativity at work around technology gadgets, but it is only a sub-component in the global system of creativity. An awareness of the macro-system whenever viewing the sub-system will prevent compartmentalization. For the 21st century, creativity would be more important since the world becomes more hyper-connected with fierce competitions, products, and service designs are clearly moving from global standardization to more of culture based designs that satisfy customized needs of widely distributed economies.

- **System Thinking can stifle creativity when management intends to control or manipulate it too much:** The problem comes, when proponents of one discipline or specialty in a subset of Systems Thinking try to overlay their methodology or criteria on another. Generally, that is when more structured practices are forced on less structured disciplines. Learning from each other is not a problem, but forced participation is happening way too frequently. Now that creativity is seen as so desirable, the management tries to artificially push it happens or pull them out of fundamentally creative-unfriendly environments or to control them. And there are whole industries now based not on being creative but on "managing" creativity.

Creativity is the most wanted professional quality in the 21st century, because it is the only force to not only keep the world moving forward (with positivity) but also making the world delightful; it is the capability human intelligence still out beats machine intelligence; and it's the superior power to keep human race thrive, not just survive.

5 Will Innovation Enhance or Distract you from Strategic Focus

Someone obviously needs to innovate otherwise the world will come to a standstill.

Innovation is the light every organization is pursuing, however, some might complain it has distracted them from their strategic focus, because a company cannot have a clear focus on everything, innovating, bringing products to market and cutting cost/removing complexity to stay profitable. Are companies able to focus on more than one thing, should their primary focus be prosperity via innovation or maintaining a sustained business via efficiency?

- **Innovation has broader scope beyond just a new product or service:** Innovation is more about taking something someone created and adding to it, changing it, adapting it; in some sense, to a particular need, whether individual, group or industry. From the business perspective, innovation has much broader scope than a new product or service, it means both incremental innovation (product update or process optimization) or breakthrough innovation (the new business model or disruptive invention, etc). It also includes "soft" innovations such as leadership/management innovation, communication or culture innovation, etc. From an individual perspective, innovation is something thrown your way in the jobs you have, the hobbies you enjoy, finding the application of a thought, an idea, a thing, or even a skill, to which you discover some practical use in the reality of the rapidly changing world. In this regards, innovation can only enhance strategic focus. Because innovation is not all about products and services, it can also be used for cost reductions, process and business model changes and improvement. Innovation is a disciplined approach to discovering and building opportunities to create new meaningful sources of value to targeted users. Innovation is the sustainable and scalable way that can be learned and practiced as a set of personal leadership skills.

- **Both invention and "hard" innovation have to pass the Proof of Concept:** What is the difference between innovation and invention. Invention is similar to innovation: Both have to do with creating something novel out of great ideas. Invention is creating something new, it is sometimes revolutionary. Innovation is adding meaningful value by improving the new products or processes (hard innovation), or harnessing creative communication or leadership (soft innovation). Proof of concept is proof of market. Investors try to mitigate the risks:

(1) the risk that the product won't work;

(2) the risk that the product works, but the market doesn't want it;

(3) the risk that the product works and the market wants it, but these people can't get the product to market.

Using external resources with internal resources increases a company's chances of truly utilizing best-of-breed talent to drive innovation and invention because the world's resources at large become open to the companies who take an in-house with the out-of-house combined approach.

- **Even creativity is a system thinking process:** The question is moot, for innovation isn't something to order up, buy or conform to the certain human application. Innovation comes from the creativity aspects of a free mind left to simmer, to think, to test. Creativity, the roots of innovation are those patterns you cannot see, cannot feel until the latent emergent behavior of the system that becomes greater than the relative sum of its parts, comes into the focus. Even creativity (the digital term "agile creativity"), the essence of the artful mind, is a systems thinking process, where you see the patterns of the universe around us, seeing some wicked pattern of nonlinear behavior by which we increase the sum knowledge of who we are, what we see, and are able to bring it to some level of understanding for those around us.

- **The holistic thinking is needed to strike the right balance of stability and innovation, run and transform business:** A successful business, or any system for that matter, finds its greatest stability when the parasitic and collaborative elements within it, find a balance. Being too aggressive is just as bad as being too conservative. Innovation becomes the 'hammer in search of a nail" for the aggressive business, destroying creativity, and ultimately much of the stability of any given company. There are axioms within system assurance engineering that support innovation as the result of many forms of engineering thinking required in order to create complex systems, such as temporal, abstract, inductive, deductive, holistic and inclusive mindsets. The actual challenge with innovation is to fully understand the system and systemic risks throughout the life cycle and the adverse event life cycle. These are system safety, software safety, reliability, quality, logistics, maintainability, availability, human factors, and system risks associated with the cutting edge science, technology, and engineering aspects, which are not commonly apparent, or known.

- **Digital innovation principles are based on collaboration and co-creation:** Innovation comes with a risk of failure, usually not well tolerated in a market governed by risk-allergic minds, protecting the interests of narrow-short-sighted benefit. Innovators should always have the greater vision in mind and strive to return sustainable development and growth back to society and the community they are working in/for. Innovation should always be involved in a "Me and the US" combination in every single dimension, stage and initiative. In this sense, altruism forms a necessary attitude and condition in today's principles of innovation, which are heavily based on collaboration, sharing, networking and co-creation systems. They should be regarded as the roots and the framework of all company's innovation actions.

Innovation is about moving forward. In any business, if you are not moving forward, you are moving backward. There is no standing still. Companies have to be prepared to lose some to gain more. They just can't have the cake and eat it; resources are scarce and limited at best of times. They have to make the strategic choices of where and when and how they innovate, whether they do that ground up by shedding ineffectual upstarts or acquire like trees drawing sustenance from the environment. At the end of the day, nothing stands still. We're all in a state of flux, and it's much easier to flow with the force that pushes up against it like the willow in the wind.

6 Is Efficiency Diminishing Innovation

Balance is the most challenging continuity regardless of the strategic emphasis.

At many organizations, in pursuit of operational excellence, there is such an emphasis on efficiency rather than innovation or creativity. Companies are focusing on improving margins by reducing the bottom-line cost rather than increasing the top-line growth. Improving bottom line efficiency takes little creativity and risk, while working on the top-line growth takes bigger risk and creativity, as it is not a sure thing. Does that mean efficiency killing innovation?

- **Efficiency and innovation just have to learn to live and function together**: An obsession with the rigidity of efficiency stunts the innovation creation process. Innovation is fluid and should not be straight-jacketed. Efficiency may easily kill the nascent and very vulnerable child of innovation not quite ready to be analyzed for its profit margin. Many process innovations will be concerned with increasing and optimizing efficiency and maintaining existing skills and linkages. The greater the efficiency of an organization, the greater the need is for creativity. Efficiency will extract the maximum benefit from a new idea. If an organization is inefficient, it will be inefficient with new ideas. "**Efficiency and creativity complement, not oppose, one another**." - Edward de Bono

- **Balance is the most challenging continuity regardless of the strategic emphasis**: As processes yielding results, innovation and efficiency can complement and enhance each other. We have to understand that the world has become multidimensional. Innovation is definitely the key to global competition, but not sustainable without a significant transformation in the organizational control thinking. The search for efficiency is also a concern for the strategic view about improvements to "operational effectiveness." New processes or workflows propagating throughout the industry, are easily replicated and will likely result in competitive convergence. Efficiency and short-term goal orientation often divert focus from innovation, which in general, will benefit in the long range, but lower profitability in the short-term. How do you address this problem as you develop a strategic plan? How do you balance the short-term and long-term innovation and opportunities? It is the art of balance and continuity regardless of the emphasis. Both innovation and operational excellence are integral components of the digital strategy. The world of strategic planning is about to change radically. Ambidextrous organization separates the exploitation of the existing methods and technologies from the exploration of the new radical or potentially disruptive innovation. Strategic planning needs to become continuous, dynamic, circumstantial and multidimensional. In other words, the strategy is no longer something you plan for, the strategy is something you exercise every single day to well leverage innovation by managing operational excellence.

- **Perhaps innovation and innovators can flourish or flounder depending on the culture-risks/rewards, constraints/opportunities:** Leadership tends to focus on culture, structure and metrics when in reality they should focus on improving communication and elaborating insight. You can't change an organization without insight, the organization adapts exclusively to the insight you provide to it. The search for the key to the "sustainable innovation holy grail" requires a specific understanding of innovators' motivation. It is not a one size fits all solution, culture heaped in control but an open blended culture heavily oriented toward autonomy with control applied sparingly. Most organizations want both innovation and the entrepreneurial spirit in concept or words but are not set up to deal with the personalities of these free thinkers through talent empowerment. People must enjoy the journey just as much as the final stage of completion, and must receive all the encouragement and support available from their peers if they are to be truly inspired to do and create innovative things.

And most of all, they must always keep their minds focused on the objective and stay positive.

In summary, the balance of efficiency and innovation is the most challenging continuity regardless of the emphasis. Innovate as early as possible. Get everyone on the same page. Think it through, execute the process efficiently, fine-tune the cycle along the trail, orchestrate the harmony, and maintain the humor.

7 Is Agile the friend or foe of creativity?

Agile stifles innovation when stakeholders dictate "how" and not get "why" and "what."

As an emergent management philosophy and methodology to run today's digital organization. Agilists are phenomenally disciplined in focusing on value, prioritizing, executing, and collaboration. Agile spurs many fiery debates such as: Does Agile improve product quality or is it the very reason for defects increases? Is Agile making managers happy, employees unhappy? Can Agile thrive in a large enterprise environment? Here is another one: Is Agile the friend or the foe of creativity?

- **Agile is really a means to realize value:** Despite the facilitation for creativity, whether this results in useful improvements is up to your organizational culture and how well people are encouraged to be creative. The spirit of creativity and innovation will be more influenced by mindset, culture, and processes or behaviors around the teams rather than whether Agile itself is used or not. Creativity is more of a culture and environment thing rather being tied to a delivery process. Agile projects that have great engagement and dialogue can be a fertile ground for creativity around how solutions are structured, designed and delivered. Thus, innovation and creativity are affected by the system at play in the organization. No matter what method you use to deliver software, if someone in the hierarchy offers up lots of "no," it will be hard for innovation to take root. Some agile practices, for instance, retrospectives, primarily designed to allow for constant improvement; or iteration and sprint review, primarily designed to allow to have customer representatives and team feedback on product increment, could result in some creative or innovative improvements.

- **Agile stifles innovation when stakeholders dictate "how" and not get "why" and "what"**: When a team in agile gets "how" in the format of a user story, they tend to look only in one direction. But when they get "what" or "why" in the form of the user story (store the accepted/not accepted value), they can think of the optimal solution. So, if agile teams focus on getting user stories in the form of "why" and "what," they can be creative and innovative at the same time. Agile is a fantastic way of working to involve everyone in the process of creation and delivery. Creativity and innovation are more a function of motivation and latitude. A motivated team will be creative and will innovate, but the team must have the latitude. The organization must allow for learning, experimentation and failure. That means you cannot run at maximum capacity. All structure and business processes tend to funnel creativity in a specified direction; Agile is no different in this regard. Given no structure and no process to follow, creative individuals have ultimate freedom, but no inherent drive to find solutions to specific problems in a timely manner.

- **Organizational culture stifles creativity and innovation, not the frameworks used to deliver new products and services:** Agile is neither a product-oriented philosophy nor an innovation-centric philosophy; Agile is a system development philosophy that assumes your customers and stakeholders know what's best for the product and for the consumer. If a change to agile methodologies has stifled creativity, then it pays to look into the motivations that drove the move to agile originally. If the move was overly motivated by solely increasing productivity and specifically at the cost of thinking innovatively, then that could be the real reason why creativity suffered.

Therefore, when done correctly, Agile actually aids in creativity and innovation. The creative solutions come out of retrospectives and collaboration within teams. But you have to have a culture that allows people to try new ideas, make mistakes and learn. As negative culture like foe will kill creativity far faster than Agile will. If the culture is always to get it right the first time and move on, then Agile is actually like the friend to aid in creativity.

8 How Should You Structure, but Not Stifle Innovation?

Innovation per se is like composing a symphony, lots of planning, but the music will come from the musicians, not the director.

Innovation is the differentiated advantage of running today's digital organizations. The gap is growing between the need for innovation and many organizations' capacities to learn how to do it. It's harder and much more painful to define your innovation constitution than to define the structures, and the formats used to make innovation happen. Although there's no magic formula for innovation success, people, structure, and process are all important factors. More specifically, how should you structure innovation, or what are the principles, processes, and practices to manage innovation systematically?

- **Inclusiveness, democratization, multi-iterations, and multi-viewpoints**: If one of your employees came up with a new initiative to start an ideation process on a certain question, where would he or she take it? That's the problem of today's innovation programs. Many of them are organized the same way as the traditional staff idea and improvement box. Innovation is so much more. You need to know how to involve employees, and how to frame the question to get the best ideas. The business knows what good ideas are, what has been done before, and can evaluate the ideas. Also, at the pre-ideation stage, you need to agree on next steps and who will be responsible for the follow-up. Fill the driving seat. Have designated staff to run, manage and curate your ideation processes. Try to include a diverse team of participants in your ideation processes as possible. Look out for curious people with a broad knowledge base, a hands-on attitude and good analytic and social skills. Make your creative processes available to everybody. Don't let individual minds ruin your innovation setting. Promote ideation near to the customer frictions. Frontline workers, close to the market, usually have plenty of ideas. However, ideation is not innovation. Keep idea generation processes separated from the rest of your innovation program. No process without a briefing, make sure no ideation process is conducted unless it is clear what creative challenge exactly you need ideas for. Ideation is not innovation. But it's still crucial. Without that constant source of ideas, innovation will not sustain. Make sure that your ideas are collected, and elaborated over at least two methodological iterations. Design your ideation processes in a way it allows you to consider multiple viewpoints in a creative challenge. Get rid of unnecessary hierarchy and politics. Politics is defined as a reflection of power balances when someone wants something, and someone else can help/block. Organizational politics can be helpful and can be a blockage, but it can't go away. It's part of relationships in human life, in and out of work. Make politics discussable and point out how people can use their power. The collaborative innovation teams are responsible that there are tools, processes, and best practices in place, which the business can use to innovate.

- **Senior leaders have power and influence, so use these productively:** They must give visible support to the end to end innovation process, including any technical support. They can also coach and mentor team leaders and speak publicly about the need for innovation. Most organizations say they have no problem with idea generation, but they under-support idea testing and wider adoption. This is where senior leaders have a role. The problem is that too many leaders do too little! Top leaders need to build a culture of innovation with the structured process in catalyzing, not stifling innovation, they have to think innovation as one of the most significant elements in business strategy and manage it effectively. Team leaders have a key role because most innovation happens in teams doing the real work. Besides the C-level sponsorship for the program and the innovation focus areas, every ideation campaign also has a related middle manager sponsor to show the crowd there is actually someone behind the question in order to increase the trust that the ideas will be picked up. Train these leaders to develop ideas from concept to implementation testing. What typically happens is that companies, after stating innovation as one of their core values, designate accountability to a Head of Innovation and feel they've done their duty. The same thing happens with knowledge management and diversity. Many heads of innovations see themselves as the actual source of innovation. That's one group. Other heads of innovations see their role to facilitate the corporate ideas and suggestion box in a rather passive manner. Ideally, Head of Innovation needs to find creative ways to tackle the innovation potential lying in an enterprise and to provide the necessary tools to unleash this creative force and to develop these tools further, with the goal to maintain the idea and innovation pipe of the company filed at any time.

- **The structure is one of the three levers, along with policies and programs, that manager can**

use to drive innovation: Remove any of the three, and you're liable to fail. Innovation is a culture more than anything, it occurs of its own volition and often on its own time scale. A defined structure is essential to managing innovation in a corporation, but there's no single structure that will work in every organization. More precisely, you don't structure innovation. You apply principles of approaches and vary the resource and tool mix by the ever-changing environment, day to day through the year to year. By default, trying to apply structure applies limits. If the structure is meant in a methodological sense, of course, the structure is needed. Many corporate innovation programs serve individual careers, not the content. Ideas are crucial to an innovation program. You need to make sure, that your company has a steady flow of fresh ideas floating in your innovation pipeline, and, therefore, you need a methodological mainframe that allows you to do that. The process to support the creation of sustainable, systematic innovation can be structured, but innovation per se is like composing a symphony, lots of planning, but the music will come from the musicians, not the director.

Some highly innovative organizations fail to capitalize on their great ideas because there was no structure in place to manage ideas. Keep hierarchy as low as possible. Cut the politics. The rigorous innovation structures are supported by the right policies and programs. There are times fostering a culture where creativity thrives really helps to drive innovation that can fit into an existing business or process. That's what innovation gurus would call routine, ongoing, or core innovation. The challenge comes with determining how to fund, commercialize, foster, protect, and focus investments in innovation that could require distinctly different business environments to prosper.

Chapter 7

Innovation Gaps and Pitfalls

Innovation fails because everyone's talking about it instead of doing it collaboratively.

Figure 11 Innovation Gaps

Statistically, innovation management has a very low success rate. The reasons why failure occurs vary widely. It is no wonder that many leaders are reluctant to act on bold ideas with good business potential due to the high likelihood of failure. It's better to play it safe than try harder and fail. How to highlight these failures so that others can be more successful in innovation than in the past? Generally speaking, innovation fails because:

- **Leadership gap**: Innovation fails because many organizations lack real support by senior management; lack the balls to invest in risk. Innovation fails because top leadership doesn't understand how to "manage" innovation or treat the decision in the same way as a capital decision. Modern managers are wimps who expect assurances and answers up front, which cause them to overly invest in lame projects and under-invest in projects with interesting potential.

- **Cognition gap:** Innovation fails because businesses lack cognitive ability to think alternatives. In addition, to get truly sustained management support, businesses need to think hard about how their function can be performed in other ways, especially in ways that they have background or expertise. It takes a combination of wacky and less risky ideas to balance out a robust portfolio worth investigating.

- **Risk management gap:** Innovation fails because they get de-risked in the development stage. Probably more common as ideas advance through the development process, they are "de-risked" to the point where they are not truly innovative by the time they are launched. Large organizations kill good ideas and thus are generally poor innovators.

- **Adoption gap:** Innovation fails because innovation without adoption is a hallucination. There is a myth that innovation may come out of a process and not individuals/innovators and the innovation is not properly adopted or innovated to be adopted by the target audience.

- **Culture gap:** Innovation fails because the culture is too shallow of a mea culpa when explaining why change initiatives fail. In this case, change being attempts to innovate new ideas. Too often people do not understand the nature of change, why it's critical for organizations to remain competitive, and how they're part of the change in order to realize positive outcomes. For virtually all for-profit organizations, innovation is not a choice or nice to have, but rather an essential function to survive in today's highly competitive environment.

- **Process gap:** Innovation fails because people start the innovation process without proper sized, prioritized platforms based on consumer needs. They may begin ideation in a host of ways that are founded on new technology, ethnographies, a cross-functional ideation, etc, without truly knowing if they are fishing (ideating) where the fishes are.

- **Emotional gap**: Innovations fail because folks fear innovation. Innovations succeed when failure is seen as a learning step to great success. Someone has innovative ideas and ready to contribute, either they are not inspired to come up with or not ready to be heard by ignoring with a tag of word weird or crazy.

- **Investment gap:** Innovation fails because, there are too many disconnects that occur between the birth of a vision/concept and the process of turning it into a reality, or lack of information actually gathered for the innovative ideas that come up. Even there are plenty of innovative ideas, there's lack of investment support. It takes a team of bright individuals and executive sponsorship to review/evaluate ideas, offer feedback, and support ongoing development efforts. An overall framework for innovation with gate reviews will help to sustain the progress and minimize the risk of idea flops. Clearly it's important to invest in the right mix of ideas (both bold and simple) with supporting business cases.

Innovation fails because everyone's talking about it instead of doing it collaboratively. It is crucial to examine the causes of failure in innovation. The objective is to raise awareness of what's needed to improve the probability of success and improve the success rate of innovation.

1 The Root Causes of Innovation Failures

Innovation is the sustainable and scalable way that can be learned and practiced.

Innovation is the light every forward-looking organization is pursuing. However, for most businesses, innovation is still serendipitous, and innovation management has an overall very low success rate. Innovation helps to tackle the complexities of business dynamic in the digital ecosystem, but often within itself, it needs to change and improve as well. The reasons why failure occurs vary widely, but dig further; here are some root causes to fail innovation.

- **Innovation as a lip service:** For many less innovative organizations, innovation is just a buzzword, everyone talks about it, but very few people, especially leaders really work on it. They still keep "the old way doing the things." Innovation is utilizing what you already have in a unique and creative way that has not been done before and using that thing to make a profit. At highly innovative companies, innovation is a crucial component of the strategy. A good innovation strategy will always be aware of strengths and weaknesses, opportunities and threats, set the guidelines and take risk-intelligent actions. Therefore, innovative leaders should always have the greater vision in mind and strive to return sustainable development and growth back to the business or society they are working for. The innovation management can be iterative, evolutionary, revolutionary, or disruptive, but it must be marketable and implementable. It is not just the new design or invention; it is taking the holistic approach to tuning it, tweaking it, changing it in a way that it brings the business benefit via mid or long term. Innovation is similar to as "the sum is larger than its parts." At today's modern organizations, it is essential for developing a company strategy that encourages realistic innovations which will prove successful in the market. Innovation comes with a risk of failure, usually not well tolerated in a market governed by risk-allergic mindset. Innovation is costly most of the time. That is why you should really concentrate innovation on the main issues of your strategy. As you innovate, you might find helpful changes to your strategy.

- **Lack of innovative leaders or practitioners:** Great innovative leaders are those who can inspire a culture of innovation, be resourceful, and have a clear vision and strategy to manage a healthy innovation portfolio, identify and develop innovation practitioners. Spotting and scoring individual as an innovator needs to focus on the individual's capabilities and potential to innovate. Creativity becomes significantly important in the age of the advanced technologies because the leaders of the future will not be mere automatons, but continue to discover, explore, and improve the surroundings. Innovative leadership relates to intelligence, empathy, idealism, process understanding, communication skills, cultural understanding, leadership, and definitely - understanding what is wrong with the status quo.

- **Poor innovative culture:** Culture is the collective mindset, attitude, and behavior. For less innovative companies, their people often get stuck in the "comfort zone," having the "compliance only" mindset, because the processes and system are designed decades ago are too rigid and slow to change, and the talent/performance management are not synchronous with innovation management. Companies of all sizes, especially large corporations, are designed to suck at innovation. Because they become too dependent on satisfying corporate regulations or protocols, and never get around to developing a culture that fosters/rewards innovation until it is too late. It takes true leadership; with less protocol, to listen to the other people in the company, in order to build a culture of innovation.

- **Lack of innovation execution capability:**
- Innovation is not a one-time business initiative or an IT project only. Innovation is a disciplined approach to discovering and building opportunities in creating new meaningful sources of value to targeted users. Look at innovation from the perspective of

developing business-wide innovation capabilities. Innovation has three phases: Discovery of a problem or new idea, designing a prototype solution and the ultimate delivery of a commercially astute outcome. That the best point of view is to see innovation as a system, capable of delivering organization-wide capability. More specifically, building a balanced innovation portfolio is a practical approach to optimizing resource and improving risk intelligence. There are many areas within a company where the innovation process can be applied to create value, including both "hard" innovation such as products/services/processes/business model innovation and soft innovations such a communication/culture/management innovation. It is a differentiated business capability.

Innovation is the sustainable and scalable way that can be learned and practiced. Because how an organization orchestrates to generate ideas, manages activities, measures results, etc, is determined by how that organization has decided to craft the innovation effort - build a good innovation strategy, groom innovative leaders and practitioners, shape a culture of creativity, and build a set of innovation capabilities. Innovation is relative and has a context. The key to innovation success is just so simple - innovation is nothing without exploration and exploitation.

2 Three Innovation Blues

The success of innovation management is never an accident; it is a thought-out planning and seamless execution.

Innovation is the core activity of digital evolution; however, the majority of organizations still uses innovation as a buzzword or treats innovation as the serendipity. They might put a lot of effort or make a big investment in it, but statistically, innovation management has very low percentage of success rate. Many organizations even experience innovation blue and suffer from innovation fatigue. So what are the root causes of innovation pain or creativity brain drain, and how to improve innovation management effectiveness?

- **Innovation talent blue**: At creative organizations with highly innovative leadership, people are encouraged and given the time and resources to work on new things that excite them, all are required to produce new ideas and brainstorm the better way to do things. However, in the traditional hierarchical organizations, creativity is discouraged and mediocrity is rewarded. The talent gap for creativity is enlarged due to the outdated talent management practices and ineffective performance management measurement. To overcome innovation blue, the workplace needs to be designed to help employees at all levels within an organization (from top leaders to front-line workers) understand and develop their creative capacity to solve problems and exploit opportunities in new and innovative ways. Keep growth mind, learn from every experience, but also learn to unlearn your experiences. Creativity starts with a knowledge base and then openness to new experience or detecting thing you didn't know or applying knowledge from other domains to a new one, results in creativity in the new domain. The heterogeneous team with cognitive differences is more innovative than the homogeneous group setting. Whether creativity can be collective is clear and flows from what seems like expansive, generous, and creative minds, how creative the team is depending on the creative capacity of its member. You can get a diverse group of people together in one room and still not have "creativity" if the participating individuals are not particularly creative. People need to be able to apply both converging and diverging thinking to ideas so that current constraints are removed. People need to be trained in creative methods and techniques, the business model is often challenged, everyone has a personal creativity objective at work and there is much humor to go around, fewer office politics, more professional learning and sharing.

- **Innovation culture blue:** Another cause of innovation blue is culture inertia. Creativity is an innate ability which is often sparked by positive attitude and out-of-the-box thinking to challenge conventional wisdom. However, in most of the organizations, people can't get out of "comfort zone," and culture inertia is one of the biggest obstacles to innovation. Here are some common responses: "We've always done it this way," "Our competitors are doing it so it must be right," "Stick to your own responsibility," "You don't really understand that problem," "Don't rock the boat;" etc. Indeed, attitude matters, and asking "Why" or "Why not," is the first step to spur creativity. Hence, it is imperative for improving the organization's culture to one that is more innovative, inspires creativity, celebrates or allows failure or prototyping. If you have or develop the right culture through change management, open, not close; agile, not rigid, risk intelligent, not risk avoiding, and then everything else can be connected. An adaptive culture makes innovation and improvement easier.

It is easier to collect, facilitate and manage ideas more optimally. Finally, if you get the culture right and people feel they have the freedom to try and even to fail.

- **Innovation investment blue**: Innovation blue is also caused by lack the balls to invest in innovation management. Innovation fails because many organizations lack real support by senior management and lack a systematic approach to managing both opportunities and risks in a structural way. Innovation fails because top leadership doesn't understand how to "manage" innovation or treat the decision in the same way as a capital decision. Businesses need to think hard about how their function or organization can be performed in other ways, especially in ways that they have background or expertise. It takes a combination of wacky and less risky ideas to balance out a robust portfolio worth investigating. Innovation fails because there are too many disconnects that occur between the birth of a vision/concept and the process of turning it into a reality. It takes a team of bright individuals and executive sponsorship to review/evaluate ideas, offers feedback, and supports ongoing development efforts. An overall framework for innovation with gate reviews will help to sustain progress and minimize risks of idea flops. Clearly it's important to invest in the right mix of ideas (both bold and simple) with supporting business cases. Innovation is a management discipline to transform novel ideas and achieve the business value.

To overcome innovation blue, the organization needs to have open-minded leadership, bright talented people who are encouraged to think differently, high-creative teams with complementary minds and heterogeneous group setting to brainstorm new ideas, effective frameworks, robust processes and learning culture to manage innovation in a systematic way. Sometimes in contexts it is like that you end up being creative by accident. But the success of innovation management is never an accident, it is a thought-out planning and seamless execution, it takes iterative steps and makes the continuous delivery.

3 Five Innovation Gaps

Bridging innovation gaps is a strategic imperative for business execution.

There are many forms of innovation - technology, application, product, design, business model, process, communication, or customer experience, etc; there're also many 'flavors' of innovations - systematic innovation, customer-centric innovation, open innovation, design-driven innovation, or management innovation, etc. But fundamentally, can you identify innovation gap and close them via tailored innovation practices? The gap differentiation helps to delineate the problems and opportunities for innovation and through identifying such gaps, a business can manage a healthy innovation portfolio effectively.

- **The innovative 'idea' or culture gap**: If there's idea gap, it means the cause of gap may have something to do with corporate culture. It is imperative for improving the organization's culture to one that is more innovative, inspires creativity, celebrates or allows failure or prototyping. If you have or develop the right culture, through change management if necessary, then everything else can be connected. An adaptive culture makes innovation and improvement easier. It is easier to collect, facilitate and manage ideas more optimally. Finally, if you get the culture right, then people feel they have the freedom to try and even to fail.

- **The innovation 'execution' gap**: Even you have many innovative ideas; it doesn't guarantee innovation success due to the possible 'execution' gap. Create a disciplined, managed space for developing and testing new models, products, and business approaches, shielding innovation teams from the organization's dominant logic, established or standardized operating procedures, which stifle new thinking and approaches. Bridging innovation execution gap to achieving the business objectives requires a contracted execution scenario with clear stages, performance thresholds, and decision-making parameters combined with an iterative, experimental learning process that supports wide-ranging exploration at each stage.

- **The innovation 'processes and tools' gap:** When the ideas have been developed or when they are able to be applied to meet a short-term objective, and then they should be pushed through an efficient execution process. Keep in mind that a new idea might need ample reworking before it finds its niche and makes lots of money and fills a need. More organizations are looking for integrations with project and portfolio management tools to ensure the ideas go straight from the systems into specialized tools to help them manage the portfolio of potential projects, and manage the execution of each. The agile innovation process and efficient tools enable the idea flow of generation, contribution, evaluation, selection, and execution stays totally connected. In addition, companies can be more successful in executing innovative ideas by relying less on silo function, and more on their cross-functional collaboration, performance management, and continuous improvement experts or change agents, who are familiar with innovation management processes and understand the horizontal, cross-functional operations of the organization.

- **The gap between 'strategy execution' and 'innovation execution':** On the one side, innovation execution as an integral part of 'strategy execution' if it involves any change whatsoever, is implicitly executing innovation; large or small, breakthroughs, radical or continuous improvement, because innovation is the key element of the business strategy, and innovation execution is significant part of overall strategy execution; on the other side, it is a common knowledge, that innovation management requires the highest risk taking at a strategic value chain, including organizing, investments, and assets. De-risk the introduction of innovations into the market, protect existing operations and brands, and establish a clear proof-of-concept before making investments to launch and scale.

- **Talent Gap:** Last but not least, it's the talent gap. The heterogeneous team with the cognitive difference is more innovative than the homogeneous group setting, as good ideas are multidimensional, they take root in unexpected places and they evolve with time and by unexpected connections. People need to be able to apply both converging and diverging thinking to ideas so that current constraints are removed. People also need permission to push ideas around an organization without the fear of failure and without the need to deliver against a short-term narrow -focused objective. Once people see things being implemented and making a difference, the confidence increases and they will become even more innovative.

Hence, innovation needs a good strategy to identify the gaps, sets up the guideline, but not too many rigid rules. It takes alternative approaches for sustaining momentum and puts more emphasis on building the balance of innovation portfolio to compete for today and future.

4 Three Barriers to Stop Businesses from being Highly Innovative

It is worth the effort to break down silos, get out of comfort zone, and prepare the future proactively, in order for individuals and businesses to reach digital premium and maturity.

Many organizations are on the journey of digital transformation, but it is the path not being fully discovered and explored yet, there are many roadblocks and hidden barriers along the way. There are also both pains and gains to bridge businesses and our society from the industrial age with knowledge scarcity and change inertia to the digital era with information abundance and innovation flow. There is still a long way to go from the classic flavor of industrial management approaches to the dynamic style of digital innovation practices. Here are three barriers on the way to stop the business from reaching the higher level of innovation maturity.

- **Silo:** The majority of organizations in the industrial age apply reductionist management style to operate the business via functional silos, with the goals to improve the certain level of efficiency. However, silos don't seem to fit within emerging 'networked,' and highly innovative and collaborative digital organizational forms, because the increasing speed of change requires frequent cross-functional communication and collaboration. Yet many business managers still apply old silo management mindsets to run always-on and always-connected businesses. The result is about the higher risk of conflict and inertia, not something the organization wants in a global business environment that demands innovation, speed, responsiveness and flexibility to succeed. The digital shift has come to a change in organizational forms away from the traditional rigid hierarchies managed through command and control styles to more fluid and responsive network forms. To improve decision effectiveness, innovation effectiveness, and digital fluidity, it's important to build a high level of trust within the upper rankings of management, share the same vision, set the strategic goals, being able to coordinate and communicate effectively across departments, and manage business performance to ensure the organization as a whole is more superior to the sum of pieces. From innovation management perspective, it's critical to break down silos, bridge gaps, and fix dysfunctional roles and relationships in order to let information and idea flow for the business as a whole to reach digital premium.

- **Complacency:** To reach digital innovation premium, complacency is probably the biggest challenge either individuals or organizations have to overcome. Because organizations and individuals that are complacent do not look for new opportunities or hazards. Some say it is not complacency that is at the heart of the resistance. It is the unknown and being afraid of new things and it will be the same for the word "complacency." A complacency mind gets used to reacting, not being proactive. If you stick to the comfort zone too long, you might lose the "mojo" to move forward and be innovative. The point is when complacency sprouts up, people with such mindset stop flowing their energy up towards the positive directions (learning new things, being creative, building new capabilities, exploring new opportunities, etc), and then, their energy more often flows down to the negative or unprofessional direction. Often it becomes the root cause of the culture of mediocrity. Numerous changes or business transformations run, complete, and then slowly crumble away as people slowly revert to old ways of doing things, while few creative teams build phenomenal long-lived transformations and make the difference. Once that complacency barrier is broken, a positive change process can commence.

- **Ignorance**: Digital is full of uncertainty, velocity, complexity and ambiguity. There is no prescribed innovation formula, or one size fits all change scenarios. Ignorance of unknown is another pitfall which could fail innovation or transformation effort. Businesses are different, people are different, and the very goal of each innovation initiative is also different. Therefore, you have to be humble to realize there are many things you know you don't know and perhaps even more which you don't know what you don't know. But it doesn't mean you should just ignore the unknown, the positive leadership approach is to analyze circumstances objectively and even predict the future with a certain degree of accuracy, to prepare the "VUCA" new normal wisely. Ignore the trivial, but pay more attention to the significant details. Innovation is the team effort, encourage all employees to provide feedback, ask questions, and participate innovation proactively, to expand their view of the business and gain a holistic understanding of innovation management. Until that happens, you will continue on the lives of blindness.

Digital premium means a lot, such as business effectiveness, agility, innovation, intelligence and people-centricity. Organizations which operate this way have happy staff and customers, superior business capabilities, strong balance sheet, and positive social influence upon the environment. Therefore, it is worth the effort to break down silos, get out of comfort zone, and prepare the future proactively, in order to transform the organization in a holistic way.

5 Three "Rigidities" to Avoid in Innovation Management

The search for the key to the "sustainable innovation holy grail" requires a specific understanding of innovators' motivation.

Innovations in the digital era are coming at seemingly much fast space, more changes and more potential disruptions, and therefore, innovation management also becomes extremely complex and dynamic. So what are the potential barriers to stop people from being creative, and how to overcome them in order to manage innovation effectively?

- **Rigid thinking:** A strong blockade for innovation is rigid thinking, relying only on how things were done before, and lack of "out-of-the-box" thinking skills. If one only looks at a problem or situation based on some parallel or formula of the past, the "options" for self-expression are limited. If the situation requires a new formula or option, rigid thought prevents the ability to create a new expression from manifesting at that moment. Narrow/closed-mindedness also blocks creativity, as to be creative, one's mind needs to be open to new concepts. The opposite of creative thinking is the static mind. Creativity requires opening your eyes to see old things in a new and different way, also learn to unlearn your experiences. Creativity starts with a knowledge base, but be open to new experience, continuously discover things you didn't know or applying knowledge from other domains to a new one, results in creativity in the new domain. Lack of humility, which is a form of rigidity and being closed to new ideas, is indeed an impediment to creativity.

- **Rigid process**: Innovation is, generally speaking, a discipline because it is a systematic way to applying creativity to the real life and business. However, should innovation processes be standardized, or is it innovation process an oxymoron? The term innovation process implies an openness to innovative ideas, with an accepted interface into the organization to actually develop and exploit the ideas as they come about. An obsession with the rigidity of efficiency stunts the innovation creation process. Innovation is fluid and should not be straight-jacketed. Many process innovations will be concerned with increasing and optimizing efficiency and maintaining existing skills and linkages. Efficiency and short-term goal orientation often divert focus from innovation in general; and innovation will benefit in the long-range return on investment. So, innovation is often dependent on business insight because you can't change an organization without insight, the organization adapts exclusively to the insight you provide to it. The search for the key to the "sustainable innovation holy grail" requires a specific understanding of innovators' motivation. It is not a one size fits all formula, and thus, innovation processes need to be robust and "antifragile."

- **Rigid culture:** If there's idea gap, it means the cause to gap may have something to do with the corporate culture, culture is about how to focus - focus on a few things that matter to the business, and the business has the capability to do better than the competitors. It's what innovation all about - do it better, faster and more cost-effectively. One of the biggest barriers to innovation is culture inertia. Hence, it is imperative for improving the organization's culture to one that is more innovative, inspires creativity, celebrates or allows failure or prototyping. If you have or develop the right culture through change management, open, not close; agile, not rigid, and then everything else can be connected. An adaptive culture makes innovation and improvement easier. It is easier to collect, facilitate and manage ideas more optimally. Finally, if you get the culture right, and then people feel they have the freedom to try and even to fail.

Innovation is both art and science. From a business management perspective, it is more science than art. Especially digital innovation now expands its horizon and flexes its muscles, goes beyond just creating the new things, and it has enriched context. Therefore, innovation management needs to take a structured approach, but it also has to overcome "rigidity" we described above and brings up the business result with agility and flexibility.

6 Good Innovation, Bad Innovation: How to Discern It

A good innovation shouldn't be just the serendipity, and a bad innovation needs to become a learning lesson.

Innovation is about pursuing opportunities by taking risks, there is no surprise that the average success rate is very low for Innovation Management. The good innovation can help the business make leaps to reach the next level of prosperity, and the bad innovation can fail the business in a fatal way. How to set the criteria, make a clear discernment, and manage innovation effortlessly?

- **Attitude toward risk:** Failure is part of innovation; it is very much an intrinsic part of innovating. Innovation is always the tough journey, not a flat road. The differentiation between a good innovation and bad innovation is the innovation leaders' attitude toward risk. It is a positive attitude to take calculated risks and be cautious about obstacles or pitfalls. Like many other things in business, balancing act to have enough failure and an environment that encourages learning from failure quickly and cheaply, without having failures that are too frequent or too expensive. The leadership attitude toward risk also directly impacts on how the business manages an innovation portfolio, with which percentage of incremental innovation practices, and which percentage of breakthrough innovation effort. For example, the enterprises are often much better at incremental innovation than radical, so they also rule on incremental innovation due to their history and incumbency whereas the startups lead on bringing out more radical innovation. With the right attitude and scientific approach, evaluation and prioritization are taken place to leverage resources in innovation management. Prioritization is about managing constraints - you can't do everything; so which innovation initiative will you take? Creativity typically comes from having some resources that you can apply to problem-solving. If you prioritize across all projects, you know which projects should get that extra increment of analysis and design effort.

- **Following rules versus bending or breaking rules:** There is the time to break the outdated rules, there is the time to bend the rules, and there is the time to set new rules. Creativity is about thinking out-of-the-box, and innovation is about transforming the novel ideas to achieve their business values. By nature of creativity, it's about discovering the new way to do things, and it often means to break the old rules or the "old way to do things." However, setting rules to focus on managing innovation effectively is also important for reaping profit from a good innovation project. Shaping a disruptive innovation to fit the market often requires strategies, designs and product introductions that build towards the long-term vision. Breaking the old rules is important for radical innovation, but it doesn't mean to be "ruleless," or get lost or lack of focus. There are no rules for how you deliver those benefits, but to begin the disruption, history would suggest that they must be offered, and therefore a good rule is to ensure that innovation efforts are focused in that direction. The right set of 'rules' is not for limiting your imagination, but for framing the system to identify opportunities and mitigate risks. The innovation management effectiveness is based on rule-breaking or making demands insight, understanding, patience, persistence, and courage, among other things. In essence, if you look at the history of market disruptions, they almost always deliver some combination of the benefits of affordability, convenience and ease-of-use compared to higher-performance existing solutions.

- **Aptitude to manage innovation:** A company has finite resources to apply to get the best yield possible to meet a stakeholder expectation. So there're always some constraints for businesses to explore the new opportunities or deploy the new ideas. The good or bad innovation would depend on the business's aptitude to manage innovation. And the aptitude is based on the set of tools, structure, and talent, which are better equipped to manage innovation by allocating time and resource to the people in charge. An overly complex process can easily stifle innovation as organizations get locked into huge processes around building extensive business cases. To optimize the innovation process (minimizing cost, time and risk, maximizing scalable solutions) requires much more effective cross-functional collaboration throughout the innovation pipeline.

There is no common standard to differentiate good innovation from bad innovation. But it's important to develop the best and next practice of innovation management, it's also critical to groom the next generation of highly effective innovation leaders with both good attitude and high aptitude. And it's crucial as well to learn from failures (bad innovation), fail fast and fail forward, to make good innovation not as the serendipity, but a new normal.

7 Five Impediments to Creativity

Creativity is the innate ability to envisioning, problems solving and path discovery. Etc.

Creativity is the innate ability to create novel value, and it is the key leadership quality nowadays. All humans are born with raw creativity. However, one's creativity strength is not proportional to his/her age, perhaps, some say it's opposite: The older you get, the less creative you become. Can you still keep the inquisitive attitude when you get older? Or a handful few is more creative than many others. What're impediments to creativity? And what're the choke points that impair the "normal" person's ability to "think" creatively with respect to envisioning, problem-solving, and seeing new paths?

.

- **Focus:** Lack of 'FOCUS' is an impediment to creativity. Particularly for most of the people whose natural bent is to perhaps be all over the place. Being focused can harmonize your brainpower with nature energy in stimulating creativity. Whether you focus for a brief period to accomplish one thing, or set aside specific times to do specific things, it's the key to success for innovators. Curiosity and a sense of adventure are parts of the creative process, and not necessarily at odds with the word 'focus.'

- **Static mind**: Creativity requires openness to new experiences or opening your eyes to see old things in a new and different way. The static mind with inside the box thinking only will be resistant to changes. The box is a boring tiny space with very little innovative thought contained within the box. In fact, everything in the box is easy to turn stale and stagnant with increasing speed of changes. Great things don't happen inside your comfort zone or in a box; typically, it's associated with convention within context. It is important to keep growth mindset; learning from every experience lets you be cognizant what is creative for you. But, also learn to unlearn your experiences, be open to new experience and apply knowledge from other domains to a new one. Lack of growth mindset, which is a form of rigidity and being closed to new ideas, is indeed an impediment to creativity.

- **Fear**: The impediments to creativity include: Fear of change both personal and in organizations, fear of disruption, the existence of chaos, nothing driving a need for creativity, the status quo, change inertia, having a limited notion of what creativity is, etc. Finding an alternate route around a roadblock is a creative act though many people would not recognize it as such. Another inhibitor is overextension and physical/mental fatigue. Emotional problems such as stress and sadness, or vice versa, can impede creativity as well, depending on what emotions inspire the individual, and what emotions don't.

- **Risk-averse**: People tend to be "risk averse." With creativity, "change" is made. With every "change," the risk is involved. The more dramatic and powerful the change is, the greater the risk would be. There is a general tendency to avoid "making waves" or "causing change." If an individual is also plagued by self-doubt, and then he or she would be even less likely to assert a creative idea public. In addition, it's easier to think and act creatively in an environment that encourages risk-taking and nurtures creativity. Creativity is inherently risky because it is new and different. Anyone or any company that fervently wants to be creative must be willing to face risks, and overcome the fear associated with such risks.

- **Personality**: Lacking in confidence, intelligence, insight and personal beliefs about one's creativity, lack of independent thinking, being easily led can impede creativity as well. Also, having too much focus on the external environment impedes creativity, as creative ideas arise from deep thought (internal), among other things. The biggest impediment to creativity is not realizing the glorious capacity one has been given to think, to question, to create, and to explore.

It comprises a combination of factors that work together, flows and fluctuates in harmony, in order to weave such creativity. To spur the spirit of one's creativity, you need to solve the problem as if that is your first problem; fit your solution to the problem, and not the problem to your solution, open your eyes, your mind, and your heart to the new idea, new knowledge, and new adventures.

'One's destination is never a place, but a new way of seeing things.' - Henry Miller

8 What's your Attitude and Appetite for Innovation Risks

The innovative attitude should be fearless to change and experiment, but be paranoid to avoid unnecessary mistakes or take a calculated risk.

Not so many people like innovation, because innovation stands for risk, and that associated with trouble. Innovation is the light every business is pursuing now, but most of the innovation initiatives fail to reach expected return on investment. Innovation is only attractive to the ones who spend their whole life thinking and building the creative stuff. Incremental or disruptive -what's your innovation appetite? Fear or fearless - what should be your innovative attitude? Fear of failing or rigid process - what are all the different types of barriers in the workplace that never let any innovation emerge? A rarer skill is being able to interpret that creative idea into a marketable innovation. Where does risk fit within innovation, and how can businesses manage innovation portfolio with calculated risks?

- **No one likes failure, but failure is the nature of innovations**: More than two-third of pre-screened ventures can't make the ROI. As more often, innovation is not just for incremental improvement of existing technologies or products; rather, it's for radically new ideas, technologies or products. However, most organizations are not forgiving to failures, as the cost of inability to bring a new idea to a successful conclusion is extremely high, even if the reasons are the culture of the organization itself. Not only the innovations wane in the process, the people championing it are suffocated and are rendered, unable to try again. So the rest do "learn" from it and never dare to try. But the point is if management of an organization can't tolerate failure, then there will be no innovation, no growth, or no future.

- **Don't be afraid of the failure, but you have to learn something from your failure:** In the world of innovation, you will fail more often, many more times, than success. So you should not be afraid of the failure. If the company does not understand the failure, then there will be no innovation. It's always fundamentally fear of failure - although it comes dressed in many disguises. You need to "master" your abilities and your team needs to master precision as a team. This comes from first thinking through the work or situation, continually learning, making "non-repeatable" mistakes and taking calculated risks.

- **Build rigorous innovation process and system in place**: The organization, especially the established companies remember the nightmare of starting out and all the risk are taken, but with unintended losses. Then, the promises are made to stabilize the company with processes that would capture and mitigate risk, so everyone could sleep well, knowing there were purposeful measures in place to protect the stability and allow for planned growth to take place. The paradox is: Trying to create too restrictive rules, borders, or an overly rigid system to churn out innovation kind of goes against the whole idea of innovation. In an established firm, there needs to be a robust and flexible process to follow, the good ideas get discussed and funded and move forward. The great attitude for innovation is to be fearless to experiment the new things and take a new adventure, but to be "paranoid" and be able to manage innovation systematically.

- **Cross-pollination is good, but makes the team accountable**: Be inclusive and give people individual ownership and responsibility for what they do. The desire to better oneself is the fuel to innovation. It's what makes the free market work. If you work hard, have a good idea, and deliver value to your customers, you will be rewarded. Without a profit motive, it doesn't work. In following up evolving stages, a small group of people with different expertise will be involved in to justify a larger scale investment, either internally or externally. Again, everybody in a team has to be open-minded and work for the common goals. It's also about empowering people to innovate by getting out of their way, recognizing them as innovators and giving them actual ownership in what they work on. Lead more, but manage less, allow people to fail, reward results.

- **Leverage tailored tools in effective innovation management**: There is a tremendous range of innovations exists. You shouldn't use the same tools or methodologies to work with human genes, and with the design of an ergonomic shovel. Any system which attempts to do that, in general, will be overloaded with its own complexity. The ideal system is to tap into everyone's skills and talents, without the typical impediments to cooperation, and relatively less creative and innovative folk can become successfully creative and innovative people once they develop or learn the system. It has to spur active brainstorming between the equal level, and it is the only way to screen-polish-further advance truly innovative and breakthrough ideas and concepts. One can't force others to think and create. It should come from individual self-esteem and curiosity, with the purpose of creating innovation-based fulfilling work and making things that people really need.

- **From finance management perspective, consider what capital you are prepared to risk in making innovation:** Risk is part of innovation, but you can manage parts of these risks. Though for innovation, it can be better not to define the budget too narrowly as with regular projects. Innovation risk management depends on many factors, since part of innovation is not knowing how and for what you will use the budget; and some innovation needs to be fed with resources while others get better by 'starving' them. If we recognize the risk we take, it's less painful when we fail. Knowing when to give up/stop is a key skill. The societal culture of "don't give up and fail not an option" really does fight the attitude needed to innovate. Never let this be so much that losing it will cripple your business, it cannot obtain the funding to continue to move towards fulfilling its core mission. That is your budget for the project- do not exceed that budget under any circumstances. Then design a strategy to achieve the innovation that can be adapted quickly and at low cost to unpredictable changes in the environment - a flexible strategy.

- **With innovative leadership, creativity is a skill can be taught and can be learned**: You want people to be able to and dare to take risks. For it is important to create a safe environment within the group or organization which encourages people to come forward with new ideas. It both encourages success and also failures (when tried their best), but discourages inaction. Next to that, it can help allocate time for all employees to spend on their ideas. And have a clear strategy which is communicated well with employees. All in all it takes the acceptance of a certain amount of risk (also define what this risk is) and to manage this. It is indeed crucial for the manager or entrepreneur etc, to give employees time to consider and develop their ideas and to be encouraged to openly explain and discuss them. People need to be allowed to experiment in promising areas of inquiry in a way that is not constrained by a fixed objective to produce a set of the outcome. That is simply because there is a great deal of uncertainty involved in the process of innovation, but that uncertainty frequently has a positive side. It is certainly the case that many innovations have been produced unexpectedly as a result of experimentation which had a completely different initial purpose.

Innovations are risky by its nature, the effective leadership, risk-tolerance culture and well-established framework, etc, are all crucial to improving the success rate of innovation and learn valuable lessons from the calculated failures. The organizations with the healthy innovation appetites should enjoy the balanced innovation portfolio with well-mixed radical innovation and incremental innovation projects. The right innovative attitude should be fearless to change and experiment, but be paranoid to avoid unnecessary mistakes, and take a calculated risk to manage innovation in a systematic way.

Chapter 8

Innovation Measurement

The measures should be oriented to justify innovations the organization needs.

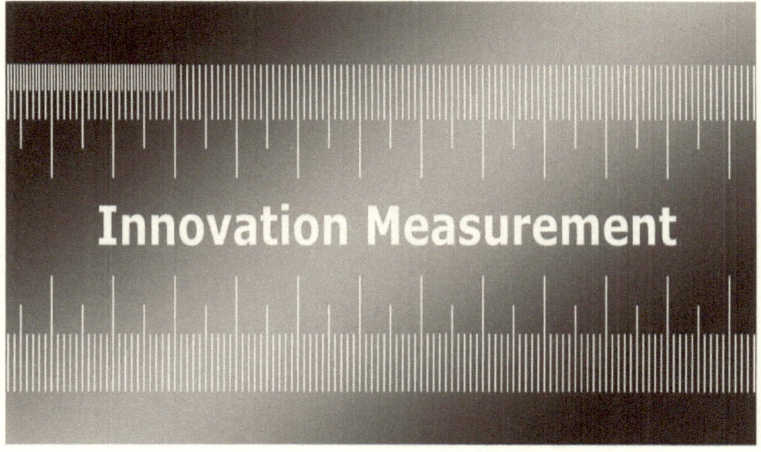

Figure 12 Innovation Measurement

Innovation is the light every organization must pursue now, but most of the innovation initiatives fail to achieve the expected result. Innovation is change, but not all changes are innovation. Peter Druck, the modern management guru, was credited as saying: **"We can only manage what we**

measure." What is stopping you from measuring top line impact from innovation, how much revenue is generated by innovations launched in the last five years? Are innovation failures caused by the time lag, inefficiency of financial systems? Is your innovation process not so clear with limited information on what has been done, or something else for ineffective innovation management, such as fuzzy or not well-communicated strategy goals? From performance management perspective, can you measure innovation effectively?

- **The measures should be oriented to justify innovations the organization needs**: The problem is often that the initiative is not well defined. Without well-defined goals, you won't have the effective plan and enough time to generate results. So, it is difficult to measure the impact without taking the time to generate impact. The approach is that the impact is generally equitable to the size of the problem the innovation is addressing. The larger the challenge, the easier it is to see the impact. Better look at what the results were prior to implementing the innovation and after. Of course, there are other dependencies, which one must assess more clearly. Asks key questions about innovation strategy, capacity, and discipline such as:

-Strategy: Do we know "Why Where When" to innovate?

-Capacity: Do we have the Processes - People - Resources to drive ideas to commercialization?

-Discipline: Do we have the Leadership - Behavior - Metrics to finish what we start?

The set of questionnaires helps a great deal to outline the total system at work in an enterprise that accomplishes new product innovation. Without this system perspective, it is difficult to identify the most critical performance indicators, and the likelihood of sub-optimizing various parts of the system is high. When this occurs, the risk of actually degrading overall system performance is very real.

- **There is no best practice solution which fits all cases:** Normally organizations look for KPIs measuring business results generated by innovation efforts. But it takes quite some time for a new innovation drive to produce those measures. One of the solutions is to define process KPIs, which demonstrate the growing capability of the organization to deliver more innovation with business impact in the future. You choose those

KPIs by deciding which are seen as critical to making progress in order to deliver more innovations. The fewer the better, but they have to be credible and relevant also in the eyes of the stakeholders. For example, culture is a perfect (sometimes it gets even too complicated) metric system to measure the impact of innovation on the business in order to unleash more successful, transformational innovations.

- **The impact of innovations on enterprise performance ranges from effects on turnover and market share to changes in productivity and efficiency:** The productivity effects of innovative activities have been one of the most challenging issues in empirical economics for several decades. The majority of studies on the relationship between innovation and firms' economic performance use the production function approach, where different measures of firm performance (mainly productivity) are explained by several independent variables such as physical capital, human capital, R&D and other innovation-related investments as well as the size of the company. The innovation studies in recent years showed that the innovation success rate is not proportional to the amount of R&D investment, which means the more money or resource you pour into the innovation initiative does not guarantee the higher ROI from innovation effort.

- **Setting guidelines for developing a customized suite of innovation metrics:** Select the few (3-5) KPIs, to keep the measures simple and understandable. There are good reasons to focus on top line vs. bottom line business performance. The innovation metrics in the context of business impact include such as, % of revenue from new products introduced. You could also change the variables and create something like % of the profit from new ideas implemented. Some choose innovation process KPIs, process KPIs could link to strategy, to make progress on the percentage of projects in the total innovation portfolio which contained a major part of external innovation. You may compare, focus on high growth markets with high margin solutions before and after implementation of the new innovation process. You may need a simple portfolio management tool and process to achieve this. The share of wealth is another interesting one to measure the change in company market value during past year divided by the change in the total industry's market value. You may consider your company as innovative, but what about your competitors/ rivals/ new entrants if they are more innovative. The goal of measurement is to create new revenue and drive early success to create a positive spiral. The change in the value of innovation projects portfolio (value of your development pipeline) and distribution of your portfolio in terms of incremental vs. disruptive, local vs. global, core vs. far from core industry, small vs. big investment, offering- production- delivery- customer experience, competitive (own resources) vs. collaborative (partners) etc, is depending on your strategy. The increase in the contribution of partners in your portfolio is the main goal of an open innovation initiative. And some say each successful innovation needs, at least, nine failures - measure the failures. If the organization allows these nine failures, it will be successful in innovation!

All innovation initiatives, hopefully, are started to achieve some business results directly or indirectly. Just measure those results. To better align innovation management with strategy, organizations must develop a scorecard to justify the initial investment in the program and the initial results (intangible and no concrete, of course) more than to measure financial results. And always keep the measurement simple and understandable.

1 Measure Innovation via Multidimensional Lens

It takes innovation to measure Innovation Performance.

Innovation is about how to implement the creative idea and achieve its business value. One can only manage what it's being measured. It is also true for innovation management. Innovation performance metrics and tools can help companies think systemically about business innovation.

- **First, have an in-depth understanding of the business "HOW" before measuring**: You need to know:
  (1) How a company is performing in bringing new ideas (Inputs) and what are the sources of innovation etc.
  (2) How a company is processing the existing and new ideas it is getting as inputs, how innovative are the processes.
  (3) How a company is bringing the ideas into reality more related to commercialization, here it also deals with profits, learning etc. (Outputs).

- **The quality of ideas as an innovation measure**: Quality of ideas is measured by how well your ideas satisfy customers' desires and how much of the idea space your ideas cover. Innovative businesses have connected their funnel for collecting ideas (which consists of their own tools like portals, ideation platforms, social networking platforms and so on) with the product development process. All the ideas collected through this funnel pass through an automated filtering and then through a manual process of selection which qualifies ideas. The collected ideas then pass through the business case preparation process. Some companies employ certain effective techniques like design factory method at this point and the results of this stage are then processed through regular design. In short, following the steps:

- Idea collection (funneling through multiple sources)
- Automated filtering of ideas (basically for the elimination of the most obvious non-candidates)
- Manual assessment/filtering
- Business case preparation and validation
- Regular product development /design/product engineering

- **The next step to drive the business and to increase creativity and innovation within a company is to introduce the Personal Innovation-index (PÏ):** In relation to this index, the PÏ will indicate, top-down, the contributed economic value of each employee (executive/management, professional/expert) in relation to their innovative initiatives and personal activities, commitment, influences, impact, and contributions. This indicator represents the innovation maturity level of an employee based on the personal impact and influences on innovation, the ability to innovate, the ability to network externally, the ability to innovation integral and the ability to accelerate operational processes.

- **The performance of delivering the ideas is another innovation measurement**: An organization's innovation performance could be measured in terms of its ability to convert the ideas that enter the 'Innovation Pipeline' into the desired output, propositions, process improvement etc. Obviously, the performance of the pipeline depends on the quality of the ideas entering it and the organizational mechanics that evaluate and implement the ideas. Simple metrics can be applied to measure the performance of the pipeline at each stage. This would allow an organization to tune its processes to enhance the performance of the pipeline and measure the performance improvement/decrease.

- **Innovation Quotient is the percentage of the total idea space covered by your products and designs:** There are several types of Innovation Quotient to measure different aspects of the quality of ideas. For example, vitality Index measures the contributing value of your new products or innovations as either revenue or preferably profit to your overall value, % of new product/service contribution to total value.

Given the dynamic nature of any organization and the complex mix of its resources, a well-defined standard set of innovation performance metrics would need to be considered in better measures of innovation success such as: revenue sustainability, increase in knowledge, impact on brand reputation, customer satisfaction and loyalty, price elasticity, even attractiveness as an employer.

2 An Innovator's Scoreboard

See through innovators from the heart and mind.

Innovation is about transforming novel ideas into business values. Innovation score means an attempt to measure innovation; so the factors included in any scoring system will depend on what you are looking to evaluate (individual vs. organization, potential vs. past performance), this is usually done through innovation indicators. What're the pros and cons of measuring innovation and score innovators?

- **Score the company as an innovator**: First, you have to clarify what/who you are referring to by 'innovator': Are those individual innovators (people) or companies/organizations/ conglomerates? How would you calculate an

Innovator's Score? Some factors that could be used to measure innovation score within a company could be resources invested (human and financial), employees motivation (top management encouragement and support, challenging activities being involved, level of autonomy given), number of projects/initiatives being launched, and organizational culture (mission, vision, structure, networking collaboration with partners), etc.

- **Innovation capacity vs. innovation performance**: At the corporate level, there's one crucial clarification: Are you intending to evaluate the capacity/potential to innovate, or the level of past innovation? The additional indicators may include things such as:
  - Willingness to accept the risk of failure
  - Creative/analytical capacity (ideation/evaluation)
  - Regulatory and/or industry influences
  - Level of customer interaction
  - The physical orientation of an office, its collaborative/meeting/etc, spaces
  - Diversity of educational/professional backgrounds

- **Score individuals as innovators**: Focus on individual capabilities and potential to innovate. The indicators to assess the intrinsic capacity of individuals such as:
  - Interdisciplinary skills and knowledge
  - Plasticity (fast learning)

- Social linkage skills and competencies
- Personality (openness to experience, tolerance of ambiguity, personal initiatives)
- Cognitive ability and style
- Intellectual engagement
- Creative problem-solving
- Ability to identify patterns
- Ability to make unusual connections
- The tendency to constantly question the status quo
- Capacity to adapt
- Emotional intelligence (risk-taking)
- Willingness to accept feedback and/or a tenacity to refuse it
- Self-awareness (recognition of one's strength and weaknesses)

- **Five behavioral traits to measure innovator's score**:
  (1) How anxious, irritable, temperamental, and moody are they?
  (2) How self-confident, dominant, active and excitement seeking person are they?
  (3) How much intelligence and curiosity do they have?
  (4) How helpful, generous, and cooperative are they?
  (5) How dependable, organized and hardworking are they?

- **An innovator's scoreboard or rainmaker index:**
  The variety of industry studies showed that the

successful innovation was mainly driven by specific personality types which they measured and called the Rainmaker Index. The other key finder is that it is the collective attributes of the dynamic situation more than the individual a priori assessment that will indicate chances of success in a shorter time frame than current methods. That means, as long as the experiences and skills are adequate, it is mainly the business or organizational environment that is the driver of successful innovation efforts. Hence, it's necessary to measure culture to make such assessment more objectively as well.

Making measurement is both art and science, measuring innovation and innovator is even more challenging. Unfortunately, most innovation indicators are flawed and present limitations. Also, the innovation indicators vary depending on who is doing the measuring, and how they are measuring, it's contextual. From individual to culture to organization as a whole, the well-designed scoreboard should motivate innovative actions, and inspire innovators to continue to push the business and world forward.

3 KPIs are Critical in Innovation Management

KPIs are critical to the test-and-learn process.

Key Performance Indicators (KPIs) are part of an effective bridge between the desired business objectives and execution of strategies. Good KPIs make innovation management more as science than art. Companies need to spend a lot more time distinguishing the "performance" of execution and the "objective" of innovation, before they try to fuse them into "the performance of innovation." Innovation KPIs can become a problem if they are poorly developed. The main outcome of adopting KPI from an innovation perspective is to improve the quality of knowledge and learn faster from mistakes. KPIs in such perspectives can be seen as a representation of what the innovation actually is (or does) for businesses - a kind of scale model or framework. The dangerous part of this discourse is the attractiveness of the "dark side" metrics and performance systems - they tell you what you want to be told. Innovation instead tells you things differently.

- **Performance indicators should focus on both business objectives and desired behaviors**: Before performance indicators are designed, the necessary and complete set of desired behaviors should be clearly established. If performance measures are to have the required impact, all of these behaviors should be assessed effectively. Otherwise, the behaviors that remain invisible will be sacrificed to raise scores on others that are being closely watched. A "good" KPI is judged both by its connection (even loosely or qualitatively) to the business objectives and by the behaviors it reinforces, or in some cases, discourages. But the even better KPIs are the ones that have been developed to positively reinforce desired behaviors.

- **The problem does not reside in the KPIs, but in the lack of wisdom on its crafting or use:** Inappropriate KPIs do mislead innovation. Particularly when traditional, operational excellence based corporate KPIs are applied to innovation efforts too early. The appropriate innovation management KPIs are more activity and directionally oriented. However, as KPIs have been used by many executives as a tool to foster results through linking "indicators" to reward and recognition systems, managers became trapped into the paradigm that a simple "indicator" should be the measurement of success for the lack of a better tool in terms of management.

- **KPIs are the best tools available for innovation managers that wish to promote continuous innovation within any organization:** If innovation managers are not prepared yet to understand the difference between fostering creativity and rewarding end results, that is another issue to be dealt with. The fact is traditional management focuses on the performances achieved upon the tangible assets; it ignores in its reporting and rewarding system for the intangible assets and resources (that include talent, alertness, vision, innovation capabilities, etc.). It means that they miss out the main drivers of performances. Reward systems that target results are excellent for "ongoing" operations where execution is the main goal. When managing innovation, reward and recognition systems that aim at promoting engagement and creativity are more important. Therefore, KPIs must be applied here too, not solely on execution. For instance, you have to change the rigid way that rewarding and recognizing through KPIs in terms of management, and pursue a more advanced performance system in the new digital innovation era.

- **KPIs are critical to the test-and-learn process**: The starting point is to define what you want to measure to improve the process. The innovation management should focus on thinking, effort and resource allocation. What's important for the business is to acknowledge that new KPIs, germane to the initiative, need to be established and these may fall outside current cultural norms and scorecard comfort zones. Likewise, for the process to be meaningful, it's vital that one is actually measuring and reporting KPIs, as opposed to just metrics. Pay attention to the dark side of KPIs, which discourages you to make mistakes. To quote Rabindranath Tagore, the poet and one of the most revered literary figures in the world: **"Where the mind is without fear and head is held high for the river of reasoning to flow, where knowledge is free."**

Therefore, if a KPI misleads innovation, it simply means that this is not a good KPI for innovation effort, it takes wisdom and practices to craft the right set of KPIs in order to stimulate advanced critical thinking and manage innovation projects and portfolio in a structural way.

4 How to Maximize the Returns on IT Innovations

IT has to build cohesive strategy, practice strong IT governance, and calculate financial and performance indicators wisely.

Businesses today face fiery competitions and rapid digital shift either technologically or economically, but most of the organizations today still focus on improving margins by reducing the bottom-line cost rather than top-line growth. Because innovation and risk are proportional, improving efficiency takes a little creativity and risk, while working on innovation effort usually takes higher risks and creativity. Still, forward-looking companies should spend more resource on innovation investment in order to reap the fruit for out beating competitors and gaining a long-term advantage. So, the question is how to maximize returns on innovations, more specifically, IT-driven innovations, because overall IT project has much lower success rate than other business initiatives?

- **Practice strong IT governance**: You need to have some kind of governance and monitoring mechanism in place following the implementations of the innovations. Many companies invest in IT innovations based on business cases that show a return on investment. What tends to happen is once the innovation is in place, there is little or no governance and audit performed on a periodic schedule to ensure it is being used as intended. Therefore, there may be some gains from the initial hype and support of the initiative although the gains may quickly decrease as time passes. To maximize the returns, put in place governance and audit system to ensure systems, processes, procedures etc, are being applied in their intended use following implementation.

- **Take proactive approaches**: Aligning IT innovation (ultimately the business innovation) with desired corporate strategic outcomes, by implementing excellent IT financial, demand, and asset management processes. Some set up the IT strategy steering committee which is part of the larger governance structure. By having a competent board-level IT strategy committee which prioritizes projects (including innovation) in alignment with the corporate strategy and then, IT management can take proactive performance management approaches to make sure that the IT portfolio is being optimally maintained through effective benefits management programs.

- **Put right people in the right place**: Today's digital workforce is diverse and dynamic; the talent may not stay in the same company as long as the previous generation. But as always, talent is the most invaluable asset to businesses if calculating ROA (Return On Asset), it has expenditure on assets in the denominator. As increasing the assets always reduce the ROA of the firm, and give returns in a long-term, management is more interested in status quo and doesn't go for investment in new innovation and ideas. However, calculating ROA only could be short-sighted. Some innovative businesses have a mantra: Employee first, customer second. They believed that if you hired the best people, offered them the tools to provide feedback, created a 365 program where employees evaluated each other and their managers; managers/leaders are responsible for the success of their employees. Turnover is extremely rare. There is the rewarding system in place for praising employees that have brought in new business or exceeded a quota.

- **Develop ambidextrous capability:** Innovation is underpinned by key elements of businesses such as process, technology, people, etc. An ambidextrous organization can improve efficiency as well as practice innovation effectively; they separate the exploitation of the existing methods and technologies from the exploration of the new radical or potentially disruptive innovation. There is no one size fits all formula, every organization has to walk the talk and explore its own sets of best practices and next practices. Balance the organizational structure with the working or leadership style of "key" people. Leadership is held accountable for employees' success, senior leadership is held accountable for management success. Think about the people first before attempting to control them with unnecessary processes, red tape, eliminate politics, open door policies. The ultimate business capabilities are enablers for maximizing return from innovation.

In summary, in order to maximize ROI (Return on Innovation); businesses have to build a cohesive strategy, to consume resource efficiently; calculate financial and performance indicator wisely. Get right talent in the right place for the right cause, -keep them informed on the same page, fine-tune the cycle also the trail, and orchestrate the digital innovation symphony with harmony.

5 How to Assess People's Creative Potential?

Take calculated risks, and reward innovators.

Traditional performance management in most of the organizations usually focuses on measuring employees' efficiency: Are they doing what is told to do well? However, digital is the age of innovation, with increasing competition and emergent business changes, being an order taker only is simply not sufficient to be a highly effective digital professional nowadays. Should organizations today also assess their talented people from innovation lens, in order to cultivate a culture of innovation and improve business competency? If so, HOW, what're the techniques or best practices can be shared?

- **Organizations should provide employees knowledge on how to identify innovation opportunities:** Sometimes talented employees are not recognized as "being innovative," because they haven't been asked to give ideas in a formal way. As marking someone "innovative" depends on many philosophical criteria, is it the number of ideas, the usability of the idea, relevance of the idea in the present time or in the future, the magnitude of the idea, implementation of the idea, etc.
  (1) Creating something new -the new knowledge starting the long road to a new technology.
  (2) Improving something or the process that makes it better.

(3) Adapting another's product or process to a new use or situation.

- **Training and quantifying innovation into measurable are also important**: Innovation is very difficult if not impossible to achieve without an organization-wide culture of innovation. The other issue is that most people do not consider themselves as either creative or innovative, so mentoring and training should be put in place before innovation is made a key performance factor. Definitely quantify into measurable for innovation such as make them attend innovation training; make them read recent trends; make them submit idea reports etc. Lower the barrier to submit ideas but ensure proper systems for follow-up into project stage gate process. Create ownership of ideas either individually or as a team member.

- **Set up a certain level of standard for assessing innovation characteristics in performance review**:
A: There most likely will be metrics assigned to a good portion of the workforce in the "Goals and Objectives" section of performance review. The innovation characteristic will go into the "Traits and Characteristics" section in a performance review. Such as the description for "exceptional" is:

a. Brings in bright, original and creative ideas from outside the organization

b. Has infectious enthusiasm for making things better

c. Constructively challenges the status quo and has positive ideas for improvement

d. Consistently acts to improve things in their own role or team

e. Actively supports and adapts well to changes proposed by others

B: The other best practice is to use the following as a method to grade an employee on creativity. A score is given between 1 and 5. Descriptions of typical behaviors for 1, 3 and 5 help to give managers guidance for picking a score, and then examples of the employee's behavior over the review period support the number chosen. Demonstrate the ability to conceive and develop unique or innovative ideas/approaches. Show originality in solving problems or completing work.

(1) Unacceptable

a. Does not develop or implement new ideas/processes

b. Seems to have the attitude that creative thinking is for others to do - has a "not-my-job mentality"

c. Often resists implementation of new ideas/approaches

d. Subscribe to the "it's always been done that way" philosophy

(2) A score between 1 and 3.

(3) Fully Competent

a. Develops creative solutions when faced with problems or issues

b. Is usually able to offer creative ideas/improvements when working with others

c. May need assistance but is typically able to implement creative processes/techniques

(4) A score between 3 and 5.

(5) Exceptional

a. Is constantly looking for innovative, unique improvements

b. Is able to work through the barriers and put ideas in place

c. Will build on the ideas/insights of others to come up with "outside the box" solutions

d. Generates an enthusiasm for creative thinking and helps others to develop their own ideas

Innovation takes place in companies with the right culture and climate. It may depend on the organization's willingness to motivate and apply innovation and creativity, and this is a different approach in the mind of the people running the game. Overall speaking, you need to make everybody innovative and make the proper rewarding system and provide the environment that hosts the stream of ideas. It is forward-looking to add "innovativeness" to the standard characteristics evaluated in the employee performance reviews.

6 The Promise and Peril of Metrics

The goal of measurement is to not only do things right but do the right things and continuously improve doing that.

We can only manage what we measure. Metrics provide feedback. Metrics are part of transparent visual management allowing pulling. There are many great things about metrics. However, there are people extremely obsessed by metrics who end up creating a huge and sophisticated set of meaningless metrics and that some managers may put a lot of energy on getting better indicators, just because they want beautiful numbers to report and not because they're genuinely interested in helping their teams improve. So, what're pros and cons, promises and perils of metrics and how to improve performance management effectiveness?

- **A measurement system is a necessary foundation for continuous improvement:** Metrics can help you get some objective perspective on what you are trying to manage, but they need to be crafted and interpreted well. That is hard. If your team or organization doesn't have a preferably simple way of figuring out whether over a short span of time, your work is better than what you did in the previous period, and created enough value for the end-users, how will you reason about where to invest in improving? Surely you won't just try stuff at random, will you?

- **Another reason to use metrics is to help stakeholders understand what is going on:** All stakeholders may not be in a position to visit the team or talk to team members, the right metrics can be helpful to track the progress made in an improvement initiative. Without measurements, it can be hard to tell whether attempted improvements make the situation better or worse. The maxim "You can't manage what you don't measure" has come to be taken as a truism. The right metric is requested in the right context but without any explanation of why it is requested, without concern for whether the gathering is onerous, or without concern for whether there is a better or easier way to gather metric that achieves the same goal, the measurement can easily go wrong.

- **Metrics help a team "fail fast" or show value delivered:** Metrics is useful only when you can act on the value. The value is just a form of knowledge when there is no action. You need to know the exact purpose of the metrics and what follow-up action is needed if it does not meet the expectation. The different metrics only make sense at different stages in an organizational maturity. Metric is a tool in the toolbox, but just because you have a hammer, not everything is a nail. While it sounds a bit cliché, it is true. So focus on metrics which help you identify trends, outliers, ask informed questions, create conversation, but ultimately you manage through relationships, not metrics. Metrics themselves won't influence the way people behave, but the way they are used will force people to change their behavior.

- **Metrics shouldn't motivate a team to game the data:** One of the biggest problems with metrics, in general, is that, once you have them, people will try to game them and they influence the mood and moral of the people that read them. We all have our biases. They are a necessary aspect of survival. However, they can filter and even distort qualitative evidence and prevent us from seeing the truth. Complementing qualitative insight with quantitative insight can sometimes give us a better picture of reality so we make better decisions and get better outcomes. Often you can see problems in using metrics when people aren't clear about what information they want to collect and how they intend to use the information to support decisions. This can lead to people trying to measure everything they can think of and display the information in every way possible, with no apparent reason for any of it.

- **There are a lot of metrics abuse and false assumptions of the metrics**: Sometimes, people are obsessed with measuring things and asking for more and more measurements. Each new measurement takes some form of time to gather, collate and interpret. There is a lot of metrics abuse. People use inappropriate metrics for the situation. People twist metrics to match their agendas or their preconceived notions. Some of those have led to metrics avoidance. Next most measurements are exceptionally subjective; they have loose logic and reasoning and make many assumptions. In some organizations, the measurements, is being measured and then evaluated. Decisions are then made on these so-called metrics that completely and utterly wrong, based on many false assumptions of the metrics. Lots of people institute metrics without understanding them or understanding the assumptions upon which they are built. Why? Because some processes told them to or because they worked for them in a completely different context.

- **The perception will come from the usage you're doing with metrics:** Assuming an organization believes that metrics can lead to continuous improvement, it won't be just a matter of explicitly communicating the intention behind metrics, but a matter of coaching and leadership to guide the team to understand the purpose of doing that and engaging on that. The perception comes not only from what you're doing with the metrics, but from whatever the team suspects you might be doing with them, including a lot of irrational (or rational) assumptions based on relationships, trust, and past experiences. Never underestimate the capacity of the human mind to weave a story regardless of the explicit communication and especially when it's overwhelmed by the rumor mill. Trust is important to gain positive mentality. Management wants people to understand what they are doing. If you want to do metrics, you want people to understand what those metrics are, what they are trying to achieve, and why you think it is appropriate in that specific context. Perhaps they will agree with you. When the team or the organization is measuring for the sake of getting numbers, you are creating waste and reducing productivity and team satisfaction.

What gets measured gets managed. Metrics are not the end-all solution to management, but simply another set of tools, data, and information. Numbers permit one to collect and build out a quantifiable history of reference, particularly for trending. Businesses need to avoid vanity metrics and really focus on key metrics that correlate to better business outcomes. The goal is to not only do things right but do the right things and continuously improve doing that.

7 How to Assess and Improve Innovation Management Maturity

Make the innovation process as visible, company-wide, as possible, but not too rigid.

Innovation Playbook Never Ends

Figure 13 Innovation Playbook

For many organizations, innovations are still serendipitous. However, serendipity can be planned into an innovation project. Serendipity is not a lucky accident, and it can be planned and worked upon. It has a lot of determination and divine providence for those who believe in that. Serendipity will always play some part in the innovation effort, but innovation is both art and science. How do you assess innovation management maturity, though?

- **Innovation Management is an overarching management discipline which needs to weave many key business factors into an innovation playbook**: A quick Innovation Management maturity assessment include:

Innovation Management Maturity Assessment	
Business Culture	It relates to vision and mission, less to innovation itself.
Leadership	It relates to business culture. The spirit comes from the top. Proactive/reactive evaluation is ok, but proactivity itself doesn't imply necessarily innovativeness.
Resources	This is really the category related to innovation. There are three clear levels of financial support for innovation: Financed as needed, limited budgeting, continual allocation.
Processes	Innovation processes evaluation is clear, but the process of "planned innovation" shouldn't be too

	rigid. Planning in some steps is ok, but chaos to some extent is necessary.
Monitoring and measuring	Monitoring or measuring is the "philosopher's stone" of innovation. However, without a positive culture of innovation, monitoring/measuring of innovation is nothing!
Improvement	Evaluate whether "improvement" relates to the innovation process or to the processes/products that are to be improved by the innovation. Obviously, the first applies, but in that case, it should be within the category "processes," because you can't imagine successful innovation process without its continuous improvement.

Table 2 Innovation Management maturity assessment

- **There are many business culture requirements call out for the standards:** How can you innovate without planning? When you have a formal innovation management system, why would you not monitor and measure its effectiveness in achieving your innovation objectives, all of which is subject to continuous improvement? Innovation process must be open to new insights that should come from the persons involved in the program. Give yourself an opportunity to envision and imagine. The truth will come out of the box. There are reports covering both innovation process and measuring the value of ideas.

- **Make the innovation process as visible, company-wide, as possible, but not too rigid:** A charter makes sense only for a company that is relatively new to the innovation process and that has not established "structure" or "culture" yet. However, this represents a solid majority of existing companies. Establish a gallery of Ideas-in-Motion in a high-traffic area near Innovation HQ. Immediately engage folks who stop and look, and invite any feedback. Let them know their feedback is valued and how. Very often, a brief chat will yield a new, interesting spin-off. Point out "what just happened," how easily anyone can stimulate new thinking, or help to validate an idea!

Emphasize that they have been part of an exciting process and to please check back often. Make a suggestion, offer an opinion. Think of other ways to include "outsiders" as "Innovation-excitement participants." "Idea-World is a Fun place!"A corporation needs the processes and culture to sustain cross-boundary engagement to discover external ideas. An internal culture is motivated to accept external ideas and rapidly integrate them into innovative internal ideas.

- **An innovation measurement framework and innovation quotients:** A key feature of the innovation measurement framework offered here is that it integrates both numerical and qualitative information that relates to innovation success. In many companies, a pervasive obsession for purely numerical success indicators sweeps aside much of the softer, more qualitative information that is crucial to understanding the health and well-being of the firm's innovation efforts. Innovation Quotients measure the value of new ideas:
(1) Tier one provides a comprehensive assessment that identifies the key dimensions of system performance and, in radar chart format,

provides a graphical overview of areas of strength and causes for concern.

(2) Tier two includes a radar chart for each dimension identified in Tier one.

These charts drill down on the critical success factors that underpin each of the higher level performance dimensions.

There are many reasons to cause innovation failure. Innovation fails because there are too many disconnects that occur between the birth of a vision or concept and the process of turning it into a reality, lack of information actually gathered for the innovative ideas that come up. If one has innovative ideas, there's lack of investment support, etc. But the success rate of innovation can be improved through assessing innovation maturity and optimizing key success factors for innovation management effectively.

8 Innovation Management Assessment and Measurement Summary

Innovation management assessment and measurement is both art and science.

For many businesses, creativity is the mystery and innovation is the serendipity. In fact, innovation is how to transform novel ideas to achieve their business value. Due to the hyper-complexity of modern businesses, innovation is also about reducing the unnecessary business complexity to tackle the complexities of business dynamic. It can be managed in a structural way. If you can only manage what you measure, how to measure innovation effectively?

- **Set guidelines for developing a customized suite of innovation metrics:** Metrics provides feedback. However, poor-defined metrics can mislead, create the other layer of complications, cause confusion or suck the energy. Normally organizations look for KPIs measuring business results generated by innovation efforts. You choose the KPIs by deciding which are seen as critical to making progress in order to deliver more innovations. There is no best innovation practice solution which fits all cases. Select a few (3-5) KPIs, to keep the measures simple and understandable. The innovation metrics in the context of business impact include such as, % of revenue from new products/services introduced. You could also change the variables and create something like % of the profit from new ideas implemented. But it takes quite some time for a new innovation drive to produce those measures. One of the solutions is to define process KPIs, which demonstrate the growing capability of the organization to deliver more innovation with business impact in the future.

- **Evaluate idea management and innovation platforms/tools:** The appropriately configured innovation platform creates a scalable means for sharing and building ideas throughout the enterprise. As a result, innovation becomes a persistent, shared reality, even across silos and geographies. A well-considered tool/platform for innovation, in the given culture, operating environment, and governance, which can be part of innovation management planning and implementation, could strengthen the innovation effort and success rate to the organization. An effective idea management platform/tools can be assessed through:

(1) Simplicity of use (friendly tool, accessibility from any devices, etc.)

(2) Flexibility to manage different discussions and votes

(3) Link with usual company IT systems used by employees

(4) Social and collaborative systems & tools to encourage discussions

(5) Transparency in follow-up a system of innovation process from the idea up to implementation!

Innovation process effectiveness can be assessed via a set of inquiries:

(1) How will it increase speed in the innovation process

(2) How will it decrease risk in the innovation process

(3) How will it effectively leverage diversity to create meaningfully unique ideas

(4) How will it effectively use the power of stimulus to create meaningfully unique ideas?

(5) How will it help to reduce fear in the organization?

- **Make an organizational maturity assessment:**
  Innovation is one of the crucial digital capabilities
  which are underpinned by varying business
  elements. Innovation Management System includes
  policies, structure, and program that innovation
  managers can use to drive innovation. Remove any
  of the three, you're liable to fail. A defined structure
  is essential to managing innovation in a corporation,
  but there's no single structure that will work for
  every organization. It depends on the level of
  organizational maturity. Trying to apply overly
  rigid structure sets limits to unleash full innovation
  potential. If the structure is meant in a
  methodological sense, then the structure is needed.
  Money facilitates innovation, but not guarantees the
  result. Statistically, innovation success ratio is not
  always proportional to the money the business
  invests in.

Innovation management assessment and measurement is
both art and science. The perception will come from the
usage you're doing with metrics. Assuming an organization
believes that metrics can lead to continuous improvement
and increase innovation effectiveness. It won't be just a
matter of explicitly communicating the intention behind

metrics, but a matter of coaching and leadership to guide the team via understanding the purpose of doing that and engaging on that, with the goal to build innovation capacity, not about adding the new layer of complicated processes and causing more confusions or problems as side effect.

CONCLUSION

Mastering Innovation in a Structural Way

Innovation = Idea executed to produce value.

Figure 14 Unpuzzling Innovation

Innovation becomes simply "creating value by solving simple or complex problems." Innovation is the process with the latent capacity to change the prevailing behavior of a group of people that initially has a stable behavioral platform. It's the way to maximize the benefits by increasing the risk when the risk is called opportunity. Innovation is production or adoption, assimilation, and exploitation of a value-added novelty in economic and social spheres; renewal and enlargement of products, services, and markets; development of new methods of production; and the establishment of new management systems. It is both a process and an outcome. Only at the macroeconomic level, innovation starts becoming visible, that's also why clustering is becoming more and more important for the business environment. Digital organizations reach the tipping point of the new level of innovation flow. Companies have always had a flow of innovation, a flow sufficient for the needs of the company at that time. What has happened is that the flow from "before" is no longer sufficient to address the business challenges of today. Hence, the importance of innovation has increased as the business has the pressure to get more and better innovation. At the tipping point, the processes for innovation will catch up to the business need. By then the flow of innovation will have reached a new level, a level that can address the business challenges.

- **Innovation = Idea executed to produce a value**: "Systematic Innovation" is an appropriately structured framework and a set of practical tools anyone can use to create or improve products, processes, and services that will deliver new value to their customers. This makes an incremental improvement, step changes and taking ideas from elsewhere and applying in the business innovation. More generally, innovation is about creating value from ideas. Making innovation happen is not hard, indeed too much nonsense it talked about this. This is not rocket science but, to be frank, it's very simple once people know management is on board and there is a process in place and some basic training has been undertaken. Internal communication and project management are key enablers of innovation.

- **Risk-taking attitude**: Many organizations are not fertile ground for ideation, they hate taking risks, and seldom learn from their mistakes; their internal politics and fears discourage creative projects by means of senseless KPIs, while they push down the innovation funnel; those tend to rely on competitors presence in the marketplace as a necessary condition for launch. They forget brand dilution, customer and consumer relevance. All of the above make the innovation practice everything but simple. Innovation by its inherent nature comes with a risk. The failure is of crucial importance in the process of achieving innovation. As so many greatest thinkers in the history have identified, people learn far deeper and more enduring lessons from significant failures than from anything else. These lessons will increase the effectiveness of your next innovation strategy and therefore probably increase your chances of meeting your objectives on your next attempt. Hence, the best judgment, a qualitative approach is given for risk and innovation.

- **Innovation must be part of the organization's DNA - culture:** Innovation is not that difficult, but this is not to say the generating great new idea is not hard. Large successful organizations once have established themselves as thought leaders or indeed product leaders often trade on their brand. Innovation will happen when people are given free space to be creative without rigid structures and without holding them back. The overriding mindset in many organizations is to discourage new ideas; leaders and managers must diffuse innovation through the organization and include everyone in crafting the innovation strategy. True innovation and sustainability go hand in hand. By etymology, "innovare" signifies "to germinate seeds." Knowing that, go ahead and innovate by inventing your future, and the one of your company's! True innovation is developing products that last long and impact the macroeconomy health widely. A useful working definition of business is that innovation means implementing ideas to create value for customers.

Innovation is expedited to adapt to the increasing speed of changes. Why is innovation important or even more important whereas technology becomes more advanced? Because innovation is the core activity of human evolution to changing the environment to reach performance for profit, for saving of resources, for the satisfaction of users, etc. The speed of change is expedited, so does the speed of innovation. Today, innovation can happen anywhere, anytime; it expands both horizontally and vertically. It's the state of mind to think and do things from a new angle; it's the business's unique capability to gain a competitive advantage. Hence, making innovation happen starts with a mindset, builds risk-taking culture, and keeps the business process as simple and flexible as possible. The creative environment is an incubator for innovation, the harmony of people and process can orchestrate the impressive innovation symphony.

Acknowledgment

Writing a book is a journey taking 1% of inspiration and 99% of perspiration. *Unpuzzling Innovation* was born in the digital era, with the purpose to throw some light on business innovation and digital transformation. Innovation is neither serendipity nor status quo; it needs to break some outdated rules, builds digital principles, and takes a systematic approach with robust, but not overly rigid processes to implement it.

The content of *Unpuzzling Innovation* is based on years of research, numerous professional debates and brainstorming regarding innovation, change management, leadership, digital transformation, etc. Innovation is its wing and collective insight is the wind. I am deeply thankful to all for generously giving thoughts and wisdom.

Also thanks for the courtesy images from **Pixabay.**

About the Author

Pearl Zhu is an innovative "Corporate Global Executive" with more than twenty-three years of technical and business working experience in strategic planning, Information Technology, software development, e-commerce and international trading, etc.

Pearl Zhu is the author of "**Digital Master**" book series (23+ books) which include the following books and receive very positive feedback.

Digital Master –Debunk the Myth of Enterprise Digital Maturity
CIO Master –Unleash the Digital Potential of IT
Digital Valley – Five Pearls of Wisdom to Make Profound Influence
Digital Agility–The Rocky Road from Doing Agile to Being Agile
Leadership Master –Five Digital Themes to Leap Leadership Maturity
Talent Master –199+ Questions to See Talent from Different Angles
Digitizing Boardroom –The Multifaceted Aspects of Digital Ready Boards
Thinkingaire –100 Game-Changing Digital Mindsets to Compete for the future
Change Insight -Change as an Ongoing Capability to Fuel Digital Transformation
IT Innovation –Reinvent IT for the Digital Age

Unpuzzling Innovation –Mastering Innovation in a
Structural Way
100 Creativity Ingredients -Everyone's Playbook to Unlock
Creativity
Decision Master –The Art and Science of Decision Making
Digital Gaps –Bridging Multiple Gaps to Run Cohesive
Business
Digital IT –100 Q&A
Digital Capability–Building Lego-Like Capability into
Digital Competency
Performance Master–Take a Holistic Approach to Unlock
Digital Performance
Digitizing Boardroom -The Multifaceted Aspects of a
Digital Ready Board
Digital Fit-Manifest Future of Business with
Multidimensional Fit
100 Digital Rules–Setting Guidelines to Explore Digital
New Normal
12 CIO Personas-The Digital CIO's Situational Leadership
Practices
Problem–Solving Master - Frame Problems Systematically
and Solve Problems Creatively
Digital Maturity–Take a Journey of a Thousand Miles from
Functioning to Delight

Pearl is a digital visionary who can capture business
insight, technology foresight, and perceive digital
leadership and management philosophy from multidimensional lenses and global perspectives. She is also a
forward-thinking digital leader who advocates business
innovation and culture evolution.

Figure 15 The author's photo

Pearl is a prolific blogger who creates a professional and popular blog: "**Future of CIO**," which has reached the over 4600 blog postings and 2.5 million views from a worldwide audience. It covers more than 59+ hot IT and management subjects such as future of leadership, IT trends, digital transformation, organizational culture and management, business strategy and execution, innovation, IT transformation, Digital Master tuning, decision effectiveness, CIO Debate, BPM, Culture Master, talent management and risk intelligence, etc.

Pearl has worked for both Fortune 100 companies to gain a variety of experiences and startup to present entrepreneur spirit. Her cross-industrial, cross-functional and cross-cultural backgrounds make her a natural strategic and creative thinker, always see the other side of the coin, also inspire her to observe deeper and broader with the fresh eyes and open mind, to become a relentless change agent, the symbol of innovation, and a forward-looking digital leader.

She holds a master's degree in Computer Science from the University of Southern California, and she lives in San Francisco Bay Area for 15+ years.

www.ingramcontent.com/pod-product-compliance
Lightning Source LLC
Chambersburg PA
CBHW031821170526
45157CB00001B/134